SENSIBILITY AND SEN

SENSIBILITY AND SENSE

RICHARD NELSON

faber and faber

LONDON · BOSTON

First published in 1989
by Faber and Faber Limited
3 Queen Square London WC1N 3AU

Photoset by Parker Typesetting Service Leicester
Printed in Great Britain by
Richard Clay Ltd, Bungay, Suffolk

All rights whatsoever in this play are strictly reserved
and application for performance, etc., should be made
before rehearsal to MacNaughton Lowe Representation,
200 Fulham Road, London SW10 9PN

The excerpt from *Ulysses* is reproduced by permission of the
Executors of the Estate of James Joyce and The Bodley Head

British Library Cataloguing in Publication Data
is available

ISBN 0-571-15329-1

For Rob Marx and Jim Ragland

CHARACTERS

OLDER MARIANNE RINALDI, early seventies
YOUNGER MARIANNE RINALDI, early twenties
OLDER ELINOR BLAIR, early seventies
YOUNGER ELINOR BLAIR, early twenties
OLDER EDWARD CHANDLER, early seventies
YOUNGER EDWARD CHANDLER, early twenties
PETER, forties
THERESE, late twenties

Sensibility and Sense is set in a summer vacation home and grounds on a lake in the Adirondack Mountains, New York State, in 1937 and 1986.

Note
Each scene has a title (a time of day). This should be projected moments before the scene and cancelled as the scene begins.

ACT ONE

SCENE I

Projection: AN EARLY DAY IN JUNE 1986, 4.05 p.m.
The living-room of a large wooden vacation home in the
Adirondack Mountains. Accessible only by boat, the house and its
various cabins overlook a large lake. Doorways to hallway and
kitchen; door to porch; windows, couch, chairs; dining area to one
side. Kerosene lamps on the walls – there is no electricity.
MARIANNE RINALDI, *a woman in her seventies, sits on the couch.*
EDWARD CHANDLER, *her husband, also in his seventies, sits in the*
chair, a drink on the arm of his chair. Pause.

MARIANNE: Did I tell you that –
EDWARD: Yes. (*Beat.*) I'm sure you have. (*Short pause.*) You
    tell me everything. You have told me everything. (*Beat.*)
    At least once. (*Pause.*) What were you going to tell me?
    (*Beat.*) I am sorry I interrupted you, Marianne. Forgive
    me. (*Short pause.*) Then don't forgive me. Fuck it.
    (MARIANNE *begins to take off her grey stockings.*)
    Now what are you doing?
MARIANNE: Taking off my stockings. What, are you blind now
    too? I thought it was perfectly obvious that I was taking
    off my stockings. (*Beat.*) Don't go blind on me, Eddie.
    Not now. Now when I need you.
    (*Pause.* EDWARD *takes a sip of his drink.*)
EDWARD: I'm as young as I ever was. (*Beat.*) I said –
MARIANNE: (*Ignoring him*) I hate these stockings. I hate this
    whole kind of stockings. My legs are sweating. They've
    made my legs sweat. It's summer, so what am I doing
    wearing stockings that make me sweat? (*Beat.*) Why did
    you put stockings on me this morning, Eddie?
EDWARD: You asked me to.
MARIANNE: Not these particular stockings. I would never
    want her to see me wearing stockings like these. Surely,
    this, at least, would be obvious to you. (*Beat.*) It would be
    to anyone else, Eddie.

EDWARD: I can get other stockings. (*He makes the gesture of beginning to get out of his chair.*) Should I? You want me to get up and get you other stockings?
(*Pause. He sits back down.*)

MARIANNE: These kind of stockings make me feel like a matron. My assistant at Bryn Mawr wore stockings like these. (*Pause.*) Don't bother to get up and get the stockings, Eddie. I wouldn't want you to trouble yourself. (*Beat.*) Not Bryn Mawr. Holyoke. My assistant something when I was Provost at Holyoke. When I was there. When I was President of Bryn Mawr, I had a positively gorgeous assistant dean. She wore mini-skirts and could she ever talk with the girls. She could *rap* with them, Eddie. (*Beat.*) Went into business eventually. I wrote her recommendation for Wharton. I did not mention the mini-skirts. (*Laughs.*) When she went for her interview she wore a grey suit. (*Laughs again.*) People. (*Shakes her head.*) You slept with her, I think, Eddie. (*Beat.*) Or did you? I stumbled in on you two, I seem to recall. Where was it – was that in my office? The President of the College's office? I have this memory of pulling apart some couple in my office. (*Beat.*) It's not a bad memory, Eddie.

EDWARD: It wasn't me.

MARIANNE: Perhaps it wasn't. But as I say, it isn't a bad memory at all.
(*Short pause.*)

EDWARD: You won't get my goat today, Marianne. So you might as well stop trying.

MARIANNE: If you say so, then I better stop. (*Beat.*) Is that a plane? She could be coming by seaplane. That would be like Elinor to arrive by plane. It would be typical.

EDWARD: Peter is meeting her with the boat. You know that.

MARIANNE: Then I guess that is not Elinor. (*Beat.*) If she'd sold the excerpt to the *New Yorker*, then I'll bet she would be the one in that seaplane. That's what I started to tell you before you interrupted me, Eddie. That she tried to sell an excerpt of her memoirs to the *New Yorker*. (*Beat.*) And she thinks of herself as almost a communist. To the

2

New Yorker, Eddie. What – (*Laughs.*) The hypocrisy. But it's so typical, isn't it? That is Elinor. (*Beat.*) One of my lawyers told me. They called up Shawn. We would have sued the *New Yorker* too. My lawyer made this perfectly clear.

EDWARD: Peter never mentioned –

MARIANNE: Who said anything about Peter? I have other lawyers than your nephew, Peter. I have many many lawyers from which to draw. This particular one you have never even heard of, Eddie. I have never spoken of him before in your presence. (*Beat.*) A very handsome lawyer too. Very well dressed. Very contemporary. And he hears things before they actually happen. Like this and the *New Yorker*. You should meet him sometime. He could teach you a thing or two, Eddie. (*Beat.*) He's a very good listener.

(*Short pause.*)

EDWARD: Would you like me to get your other stockings? I would, you know.

MARIANNE: Eddie, I know you would do anything in the world for me.

(*He smiles to himself.*)

You're smiling.

(*He stops smiling.*)

You haven't stopped smiling since I told you that Elinor was coming up.

EDWARD: You didn't tell me. She called me.

MARIANNE: You didn't tell me that.

EDWARD: Yes, I did.

(*Pause.*)

MARIANNE: What did she do – call you up for more alimony? That's what I would do in her shoes – bleed you dry with alimony. (*Beat.*) Perhaps we should get divorced, Eddie.

(*He smiles to himself. She smiles. Short pause.*)

Is my wig straight? I would hate to have her see me with a crooked wig. Would you tell me if my wig wasn't straight, or just let me humiliate myself, Eddie?

(*They look at each other. He turns away.*)

The last time I saw her she'd gained weight. (*Beat.*) Say
something about the wig. Pay me a compliment. Don't
you think I need to hear compliments? The fact that I will
no longer believe them doesn't mean I don't want to hear
them, Eddie. (*Short pause.*)
If she pities me, I'll spit in her face.
(EDWARD *sort of twitches in his chair, then rubs his face.*)
That got a reaction out of you. (*Laughs to herself.*) A tuft of
hair is growing back. That's something. I noticed this
morning.
(*Short pause as she listens.*)
I don't hear the boat. What I heard wasn't our boat.
(*Beat.*) I nearly bought another wig. What a beautifully
gorgeous wig it was. The colour I have always wanted to
have. I had my purse out and I was paying for that wig.
(*Beat.*) The clerk should have told me first it was made in
South Africa. It wasn't my fault he'd gone ahead and
fitted it. I'd said I wanted it, but I hadn't paid for it.
Clerks should know better. One still has one's beliefs even
when one is bald-headed. (*Beat.*) At least I do mine.
(*Beat.*) You'd have been proud of me, Eddie. (*Beat.*) That
clerk was sorry I ever walked through his door. (*Beat.*)
That I had ever come through his door. Been brought
through – (*Short pause.*) I had fun at least. He was so
angry he didn't pity me. And he didn't seem to want to
talk about South Africa at all. Like so many young people
today. Don't you think, Eddie? (*Beat.*) Young people
today – (*Pause.*)
How many drinks have you had since lunch? How are you
going to defend me? Once in my life I need your help and
look at you.
(*He looks at her.*)
Nah. You don't look so bad.
(*He smiles.*)
No. You don't, dear.
(*Noise off.*)
There's the boat. I hear the boat. Elinor's here.
(*Pause.*)

4

SCENE 2

Projection: AN EARLY DAY IN JUNE 1937, 4.40 p.m..
Setting the same. MARIANNE RINALDI, *early twenties – the*
Marianne of the previous scene nearly fifty years earlier – sits on the
couch. EDWARD CHANDLER, *also early twenties, sits in the chair.*
ELINOR BLAIR, *early twenties, sits on the arm of the couch.*

EDWARD: Marianne, he's our host. He invited us. We just got
    here.
MARIANNE: He invited you, Eddie. You invited us.
EDWARD: (*To* ELINOR) Elinor, you talk to her. When I said I
    wanted to bring two colleagues from the *Review*, he –
MARIANNE: (*To* ELINOR) Did he say 'colleagues', or did he say
    'girls'?
EDWARD: I said 'colleagues'. (*Beat.*) I of course said
    colleagues'. (*Beat.*) Maybe I said 'female colleagues'.
MARIANNE: Jesus Christ, what did I tell you?
EDWARD: (*To* ELINOR) And he said that was fine! Bringing you
    two was fine with him. (*To* MARIANNE) So damn it you
    were invited!
MARIANNE: Why does none of this surprise me?
    (ELINOR *smiles.*)
EDWARD: Look, if you're going to make up your mind before
    we even talk with Gene – (*Beat.*) Then I'll shut up. (*Beat.*)
    You want me to shut up, I'll shut up.
MARIANNE: Shut up. You interrupted my story.
    (*She turns to* ELINOR.)
EDWARD: You won't even give him a chance?
    (*Short pause.*)
    Just because he happens to be rich? (*Beat.*) Who's the real
    snob there?
    (*Short pause.*)
MARIANNE: (*To* ELINOR, *ignoring* EDWARD) So we were
    getting off the boat –
EDWARD: Damn it, there is just one thing I want to say!
    (*Pause.* MARIANNE *and* ELINOR *do not look at him.*
    Finally, he goes to the porch door, opens it and goes out. The

5

door slams. Immediately he comes back in, goes to the little bar
set up on a counter top, and begins to pour himself a drink.)

MARIANNE: So we were getting off the boat. And Mr Hopkins
– (*Beat.*) Eddie's good friend, Gene-the-millionaire-
Hopkins. I mean look at this place. The money it must
take to just maintain the grounds – (*Beat.*) You know
Eddie's spent the last two summers up here with his pal,
Gene. (*Beat.*) Eddie better be careful or he's going to start
to think like a rich person. Even think he is a rich person.
He better be careful. He better –

ELINOR: Marianne, please. (*Short pause.*) So Gene is there and
we are getting off the boat.

MARIANNE: Gene is helping me off the boat; and it was so
obvious, Elinor, that this man is staring at my legs. In
fact, he doesn't even try to hide the fact that he is staring
at these legs. (*Beat.*) Maybe he's thinking, Eddie, that he
can afford to buy these legs.

EDWARD: Oh, for Christ's sake!
(*Short pause.*)

ELINOR: You have nice legs, Marianne.

MARIANNE: Thank you. You have nice legs too, Elinor. Don't
disparage your legs.

ELINOR: I wasn't –

MARIANNE: Anyway, we are now walking up from the dock,
and he turns and says: 'Does Imperialist Japan mean
anything to you?'

EDWARD: I doubt if Gene just turned to you and said –

MARIANNE: He did. I swear.

ELINOR: Unbelievable.

MARIANNE: Not really. Not for a rich boy. You expect this
kind of thinking from a rich boy.

EDWARD: What kind of thinking?! So he just asked –

MARIANNE: Elinor understands.

ELINOR: I understand.

MARIANNE: So. A rich boy. (*Beat.*) And I say – 'Imperialist
Japan? Why sure, Mr Hopkins. I hate old Imperialist
Japan. What kind of girl do you take me for?' I'm
exaggerating, but almost that. But it is just so obvious that

he thinks he's being so political with me by throwing around this 'Imperialist Japan'.

ELINOR: (*To* EDWARD) Just like with the Williams boys. You could always tell a Williams boy at Smith. It was like they'd just read a newspaper in the car on their way to Smith.

MARIANNE: Or a Dartmouth boy.

ELINOR: Or a Dartmouth boy.

MARIANNE: But I still don't know exactly what Gene is getting at when – and this is amazing – it gets better – or worse – and he says to me – 'Silk'. And there he is staring down at my legs again. (*Beat.*) I'm beginning to wonder if it's just not some affliction with his neck – it is that obvious – when I realize he is referring to my stockings. I was wearing these silk stockings.

ELINOR: I remember.

MARIANNE: I took them off a little while ago. They were very hot. (*Beat.*) And he says to me: 'Marianne – you don't mind if I call you Marianne, do you?' (*Beat.*) 'Of course not – Gene.'
(*She laughs.*)

EDWARD: (*Without anyone really listening to him*) He's a very good man. He's as far to the left as –

MARIANNE: He says: 'I hope I won't offend you by saying that most *progressive* women – these days – wouldn't be caught dead wearing anything silk. Because of –' And I chime in – 'Imperialist Japan. Of course, I know that.' (*Beat.*) Well actually, I didn't. Did you?

ELINOR: No.

MARIANNE: I don't remember anyone at Smith saying a word against wearing silk.

ELINOR: And the women at Smith are progressive if they are anything. (*To* EDWARD) It's not exactly Vassar, after all.

MARIANNE: Well – I made it very clear that I am progressive. That I am more than just progressive. I tell him if he knew me better he'd see just how ridiculous it was to even suggest that I wasn't.

EDWARD: (*To himself*) He's helped a lot of people. He knows a lot of people. A lot of smart, political, good people.

MARIANNE: But anyway, this is what I said to him. This is what I've been getting to. I take him by the arm – I put my arm in his arm – and: (*Beat.*) 'Gene, when I saw you staring at my legs down on the dock, I thought to myself, what a dull, juvenile, selfish, spoiled rich-boy creep.' (*Beat.*) 'How relieved I am to find that that leg stare was meant – politically.'
(*She and* ELINOR *laugh.*)
Then: 'Yes. Yes,' he says. 'I'm glad you understand that. A political stare. Not uncommon for me really.'
(*They laugh, suddenly* ELINOR *starts laughing louder.*)
What? What?!

ELINOR: (*Laughing*) I just remembered, that on the dock, Gene took a good long look down my dress. He must have thought my chemise was silk!
(*She laughs hard.*)

MARIANNE: You just remembered that?

ELINOR: (*Laughing*) Yeh.

MARIANNE: It happens to you that often, that it just slipped your –?

ELINOR: (*Laughing*) Yeh.

MARIANNE: Oh.
(MARIANNE *makes herself laugh with* ELINOR. *Finally they finish.*)
We're done now, Eddie. (*Beat.*) Now you can say whatever you want. Even defend your good buddy, Gene – if you want.

EDWARD: Gene doesn't need me to defend him.

ELINOR: (*Laughing*) I think he should take whomever he can get.

EDWARD: And certainly not from you two. His commitment to the left –

MARIANNE: Oh, please. You mean to the left breast?
(MARIANNE *and* ELINOR *laugh almost hysterically now.*)

EDWARD: But if you need to attack him before you can ask him for money – if that's what this is about – that's your problem.

8

MARIANNE: (*Calming down*) I'm not asking him for money.
　　　The *Review* is. (*Beat*.) And even that wasn't my idea.
　　　(*Pause.* MARIANNE *wipes her eyes*.)
　　　I don't know when I've laughed so hard. Ow. I hope I
　　　haven't hurt myself.
　　　(*They laugh again*.)
ELINOR: What do you say we go for a swim?
MARIANNE: (*Getting up*) Great idea. You remembered to bring
　　　a suit? (*To* EDWARD) Or would Gene rather we didn't
　　　wear bathing suits? Perhaps that would clinch his
　　　support.
ELINOR: Marianne.
　　　(*Short pause.* EDWARD *looks away*.)
　　　I brought my suit. (*To* EDWARD) Though I haven't worn
　　　it since Smith. I hope it still fits.
MARIANNE: I thought you loved to swim.
ELINOR: I do, why?
MARIANNE: You just said you hadn't been swimming since
　　　Smith.
ELINOR: Marianne, I said I hadn't worn it since Smith.
　　　(ELINOR *laughs,* MARIANNE *laughs*.)
EDWARD: (*As* ELINOR *and* MARIANNE *leave through the porch
　　　door*) Gene said he'll see us about six. (*Beat*.) We make our
　　　proposal at six!
　　　(*From off, they laugh. Pause*.)

SCENE 3

Projection: 4.55 p.m.
1986. Setting the same. EDWARD *is still in the chair, drink to his
side.* MARIANNE *is on the couch as in scene 1. The porch door has
just opened and* ELINOR BLAIR, *in her seventies, is in the doorway*.

ELINOR: Don't get up. Please.
EDWARD: (*Turning to the door*) Elinor! We were beginning to
　　　wonder. We heard the boat ages ago.
ELINOR: I was washing up in my cabin.

(*She looks at* MARIANNE *who is not looking at her.*)
Don't get up, Eddie. Sit down. Eddie –
(*He is up and goes to hug her.*)

EDWARD: You look wonderful.

ELINOR: And you.
(*Beat. They hug.*)
And you.

EDWARD: (*Moving to the bar*) Take my chair. What is it, Scotch or Bourbon this year?

ELINOR: Later. My stomach. (*Looks at* MARIANNE.) The ride – I'd forgotten what it was like when the water was choppy. My stomach. (*Beat.*) As you both know, I always have had a delicate stomach.
(MARIANNE *laughs to herself.* EDWARD *pours himself a drink.*)

EDWARD: One for me then.

MARIANNE: Eddie.

EDWARD: (*Ignoring her*) Well, the place hasn't changed. (*Beat.*) At least that hasn't changed.

ELINOR: Still no electricity?

EDWARD: Across the lake they have it now.

ELINOR: I hope you never get it here. It would be so different. (*Short pause.*) And to think that George and I could have – And at that price. You were the smart ones, let me tell you. (*Beat.*) But I wasn't like George; I didn't blame you. If it hadn't been friends, it would have been strangers. Old man Hanson asked us first. If we wanted to blame anyone, we should have blamed ourselves. (*Beat.*) There are buyers in this world and there are renters. Good for you. It must be a gold mine now. You must get offers all the time. (*Beat.*) The summers here with George, I shall always –

EDWARD: I haven't gotten any offers, Elinor. It's not Manhattan. You want to make an offer?
(*Short pause.*)
Marianne, have we gotten a single offer for this place?
(MARIANNE *lifts her head and looks at* EDWARD.)

ELINOR: (*To* MARIANNE) Hello, dear. How are you feeling?

(*Short pause.*)

That's a gorgeous wig.

(MARIANNE *suddenly turns to* EDWARD *and looks at him.*)

EDWARD: It's on straight.

(*Short pause.*)

ELINOR: How lucky you are to have such a peaceful relaxing
place to – get better in. (*To* EDWARD) It was such a shock
when I heard. You can imagine how it seemed – after
going through it all with George just last –

EDWARD: Marianne is sitting right there, Elinor.

(*Pause.*)

ELINOR: I would like a Scotch please, Eddie.

(*He goes to pour her a drink.*)

(*Finally, to* MARIANNE) We've been best friends since –

MARIANNE: Eddie, where's my lawyer? (*Beat.*) I thought I
made myself perfectly clear that I wanted him here. What
does he think I pay him for? We feed him. He spends the
day fishing.

ELINOR: Peter's in my cabin.

MARIANNE: My lawyer, and already she's calling him –

ELINOR: (*To* EDWARD) He said he wanted to make my bed. I
told him –

MARIANNE: (*To* EDWARD) I asked you to make her bed. You
promised me you'd make it. This morning you promised.
If you had kept your promise it would be made!

(*Pause.* MARIANNE *turns away.*)

ELINOR: (*Taking the drink from* EDWARD) Thank you. (*Beat.*)
Where in the world did you find a lawyer who makes
beds, drives motorboats –? All my lawyers seem to know
how to do is have lunch.

(*She laughs. No one else does.*)

EDWARD: Peter is my nephew.

ELINOR: Ah. (*Beat.*) You always knew how to make a drink. I
say if you can't taste it . . .

EDWARD: Peter should be here any minute. It can't take that
long to make a bed.

MARIANNE: (*Without looking at him*) How would you know?

EDWARD: We can talk when Peter gets here.

(*Long pause. They wait.*)

ELINOR: (*Suddenly standing*) Oh, let's not talk yet! After all I'm
not here just to talk, but also to visit. In fact, I think that's
why I'm really here – to visit. (*Beat.*) I could have talked
through my lawyer.

(MARIANNE *laughs.*)

Why are you laughing, Marianne? (*Beat. To* EDWARD) I
know what she thinks. Marianne, you cannot be further
from the truth. My lawyers told me your case was
ridiculous. They said they'd never seen such a waste of
time. They begged me not to give it another thought.
(*Short pause.*) Most people find it rather pathetic actually.
(*Beat.*) I'm sorry to tell you this, but they do. I thought it
best if I were the one to tell you this. That is why I came.
And did I come with a lawyer? Do you see *me* with a
lawyer, Marianne?

(*Short pause.*)

Don't talk to me. Use your illness against me.

(*Pause.*)

EDWARD: Would you like a snack? Can I get you anything?
That is, if your stomach –

ELINOR: Not one of our friends blames me. I only wrote what I
remembered. I didn't write history. So write what you
remember, Marianne. I won't sue you for libel. Why
don't you settle it that way? Write what you want.
Remember what you want. (*Short pause.*) The one thing I
do not appreciate is the begging for sympathy. That has
hurt me. I have never seen someone use an illness like –
(*Beat.*) You'd never have seen me act this way, if I were
the one – (*Beat. To* EDWARD) There are friends of ours
who won't even talk to me!

(*Pause.*)

MARIANNE: Really? Did you hear that, Eddie?

(*She smiles.*)

ELINOR: I spent the whole of last year at George's side. I resent
this, this – (*Starts to choke up.*) I'm sorry. (*She goes back
and sits in the chairs. Then forcefully to* MARIANNE) I can't
sit here and take this! Marianne, dear, how are you? No

matter how you behave towards me I am still happy to see you. (*Almost crying*) No matter how much you try to hurt me. I – (*She cries. Beat. To* EDWARD) I love her. She can't make me not love her. (*She continues to cry. Pause.*)

MARIANNE: Look at her starting already, Eddie. I told you she'd start with crying. (*Beat.*) That she'd try crying first. Please, Eddie, I am feeling very tired – or is it bored – all of a sudden. I think I'd like my nap now.

(EDWARD *goes to pick her up.*)

ELINOR: Let me get Peter to help.

MARIANNE: My husband will carry me. Thank you.

(*With effort he picks her up.*)

(*To* EDWARD) If you drop me in front of her . . .

(*He smiles.*)

Watch the wall. Eddie, watch it!

(*He smiles again.*)

(*As they go*) Hold me tighter.

(*They go down the hallway.* ELINOR *stops sobbing, wipes the tears from her eyes. She gets up and gets her purse, opens it, takes out make-up which she starts putting on while watching herself in a small mirror. We watch for a while as she does this.*)

SCENE 4

Projection: 5.55 p.m.

1937. *Setting the same.* MARIANNE *sits on the couch; as she speaks, she looks through a pile of papers and files on which she makes notes.*

MARIANNE: (*In a loud voice*) Fact: the *Leftist Review* was founded by members of the Communist Party, yes, but not by the Party itself. (*Beat.*) Fact: financial support for the *Review* came not directly from the Party but rather indirectly through a guaranteed pre-sale to John Reed Clubs.

ELINOR: (*Off, in the kitchen*) Good point!

13

MARIANNE: (*In a loud voice*) This arrangement then can be seen as nothing more than that say between a publisher and a book club. (*Beat.*) Nothing more!

ELINOR: (*Off*) I like it!

MARIANNE: (*In a loud voice*) And though elements within the Party still claim we have stolen the *Review* out from under them, all we in fact have done is tear up a contract between a publisher and a book club.

ELINOR: (*Off*) Clever girl!

MARIANNE: (*In a loud voice*) And fact: I promise you – we promise you – that our plans for the *Review* include no attacks upon either the Party or Party members; just because we are attacked will not mean that we shall in turn attack our attackers.

ELINOR: (*Entering with a tray with dishes and a tin of biscuits*) That should relieve Mr Gene Hopkins' mind.

MARIANNE: (*Turns towards* ELINOR) Just in terms of common sense, why would we want to take on the Party? We all after all do have the Party in our recent past. (*Turns back and looks through the papers.*) Why fan the flames? We have other fish to fry, as my colleagues will soon tell you. But first to put this concern to eternal rest –

EDWARD: (*Entering from the porch*) He's not around the boat house. I don't know where he is.

ELINOR: It's not six.

MARIANNE: We would never dream of involving ourselves let alone a friend such as yourself in a direct conflict with the Party. We've all seen where that leads. We are all progressives here, yes, but we are also all practical people. And as practical people we are perfectly aware that a man such as yourself, Mr Hopkins, who is known to support numerous progressive causes, would not want to find himself funding one which attacks another. This is not going to happen. It will not happen. You have our word. (*Beat.*) That's my speech. (*She sticks her fingers in her mouth pretending to gag herself.*)

ELINOR: Right. I know what you mean.

EDWARD: You know what what means?

ELINOR: Grovelling, Eddie. Grovelling. Have a biscuit, they were on the counter in the kitchen. They're imported.

MARIANNE: Of course. Some import revolution, others import –

EDWARD: I'm not grovelling. And I have no intention of grovelling. And as far as I can tell, Gene isn't asking us to –

MARIANNE: (*Getting up*) Anyone else want a Manhattan? (*She goes to the bar.*)

EDWARD: As a matter of fact, I would.

MARIANNE: (*To herself*) Why did I ask? Elinor? (ELINOR *shakes her head.*)

EDWARD: I have had one drink. (*Beat.*) Two drinks all afternoon. No more.

MARIANNE: So who's counting? (*Short pause.*)

ELINOR: After Marianne, then it's your turn, Eddie.

EDWARD: You know what I'm going to say. (*Pause.*) I'm going to say that *we* think it's now time to go *with* history and all that that means.

MARIANNE: Which is?

EDWARD: Come on, you've heard me talk about this a hundred times.

MARIANNE: Never like this though. Never watching you getting set to fall on your knees and beg some rich turkey for money.

ELINOR: Marianne –

MARIANNE: No. It just sounds different in this context. It sounds like bullshit. Vague general bullshit! Here's your drink. (*She hands him his drink. Short pause.*)

EDWARD: What did I do? (*Beat. To* ELINOR) What has gotten into her?

ELINOR: You know, she's –

EDWARD: No, I don't. (*Pause. Suddenly slams his drink down.*) I said I don't know!! (*Short pause.*) Look, I'm trying to do something here. If you don't want to participate, fine. That's your decision. OK? (*Beat.*) OK?!! Go lock yourself

15

in your cabin if you want, I don't care!! (*Beat.*) Just get off
my back, Marianne! I am trying to do something. Is this
clear? It's not easy. But that doesn't mean it shouldn't be
done. At least that's what I think. (*Short pause. To*
ELINOR) How was the swimming?

ELINOR: Fine.

EDWARD: Water wasn't too cold?

ELINOR: No. (*Beat.*) You spilled some of your drink.
(*Beat.*)

EDWARD: Yes.
(*Beat. He takes out his handkerchief and begins to wipe up the
spill.*)

MARIANNE: Elinor, do you have your sun cream with you? I
think my shoulders really got burned.

ELINOR: It's in my purse. (*Beat.*) Next to Eddie.
(*Short pause.* MARIANNE *finally goes and gets the purse. She
takes out the cream, and during the next few minutes puts the
cream on her shoulders.*)
It's after six.

EDWARD: As I was saying, I will talk about how we need now
to go *with* history.
(MARIANNE *at a distance laughs to herself. Pause.* EDWARD
continues.)
Go where history takes one, we mean. An ideology
basically holds one back, we think. It helps you explain
some things, sure – there is good, some good there, this –
the *Review* – will not be an attack on ideologies.

MARIANNE: Without some sort of ideology, how are you going
to choose what you will and what you will not publish?
(*Beat.*) Upon what will you base choice? What are your
criteria? (*Beat.*) Speaking as Gene now, of course.

EDWARD: Of course. (*Beat.*) OK. OK. (*Short pause.*) Speaking
to Gene. We will publish what *we* believe is worth
publishing. We will select on the basis of merit – artistic,
intellectual – both with regard to the writing and the
writer. We feel that without the Party or any other strong
ideological force on our backs – so to speak – the range of
writing we can –

MARIANNE: You mean by taste then?

EDWARD: No – Gene, not simply by –

MARIANNE: By taste. Call it what you want but that's what it amounts to, Eddie. Taste derived from your bourgeois upbringing.

ELINOR: I don't think Gene would talk like –

MARIANNE: Taste formed by your reactionary cultures. Tastes like these don't change by themselves. Without the spine of beliefs –

EDWARD: We have beliefs.

MARIANNE: Without ideology, such beliefs are based on what? More tastes? More tastes derived from the same –

EDWARD: Not tastes! Consciences! Minds! Opens minds!

ELINOR: Hey you two –

EDWARD: This will tell us what to and not to publish. What we know in our hearts and stomachs to be good writing!

MARIANNE: What you and these two girls agree to be good!

EDWARD: Initially yes!

MARIANNE: What you three agree about?!

EDWARD: Yes!

MARIANNE: So you need to agree? I thought you stood *for* argument? I thought you stood for debate and disagreement! I thought after the way you were speaking, I was going to hear how you have brought union leaders on to your editorial board. And garment workers and Italian bricklayers. And coloured maids! (*Beat.*) And also Republican farmers and small shopkeepers. Why not fascists and Klansmen as well? I thought all the world under the sun to debate and argue until reason and truth and justice will out?! And all without ideology! All pure. All honest. All good. (*Beat.*) But now I hear that it's really all up to you three middle-class minds. What you like and don't like. You three peas in a pod, so to speak. Why, in six months I wouldn't be surprised if you three found yourselves going to the bathroom at the same time. (*Long pause.* EDWARD *drinks.* ELINOR *thumbs through papers.*) Hey, come on, I was only being Gene.

17

ELINOR: (*Ignoring her*) We should get the editorial statement out. We should have him look at that.

MARIANNE: Hey.

(*She goes to* ELINOR *and suddenly pulls open* ELINOR'*s blouse and looks down at her breasts.*)

ELINOR: (*Pushing* MARIANNE *away*) What are you doing?

MARIANNE: I was only being Gene.

(*She laughs.* ELINOR *ignores her.*)

ELINOR: The statement. (*Reads:*) 'In a world that is changing blah blah blah . . . It is the hope of the editors blah . . . a forum for free thought, debates, blah, etc.' (*Beat. To* EDWARD) It reads well. We should read it out loud to him.

(*Pause.*)

EDWARD: (*Looking at no one*) It is so goddamn easy to be negative. It's so easy. Fuck!!!

(*Short pause. Suddenly he stands and goes to* MARIANNE. *He grabs her by the front of her dress.*)

Gene, you're not Jewish, are you?

ELINOR: Eddie!

EDWARD: I'm talking to Gene!

(*Beat. He lets go of* MARIANNE.) You're not Jewish, are you? Well, neither am I. In fact my father's a minister. The Chaplain of Hamilton College. None of us three here is Jewish. (*Beat.*) But imagine for a moment that you are Jewish. And if you're like the Jews I know, you've been brought up – your parents brought you up – progressive. (*Beat.*) Maybe even to the left of progressive. Maybe even communist. Certainly socialist. The world socialist revolution – the notion or idea of such a revolution – is no stranger to you.

MARIANNE: So what?

EDWARD: So you have a set of beliefs. You are under the umbrella of an ideology. You know how the world should be, and how such a world should and will happen. (*Pause.*) Now, imagine you are Jewish – this same Jew – and you hear about this Chancellor Hitler and about all the things he's been saying about you. (*Beat.*) Not

specifically about you. But about you. (*Beat.*) The priority
– what had been your priority of world revolution – begins
to pale when set side by side with this next threat. It
becomes clearer and clearer what must be done. Where
one must put one's energies. It is after all now not a
question of justice but of survival. (*Short pause.*) Now an
ideology – a party – which does not allow for the flexibility
to change priorities, to recognize and target new and
different threats, I feel, fails its followers. Leaves them
abandoned in a world which moves in such unpredictable
directions. (*Short pause.*) Perhaps no ideology can avoid
being rigid. Perhaps this is the failing of all ideologies. I
don't know. All I do know is that we must encourage
people to question not only what they've been taught or
brought up to question, but what their experience of the
world, their own common sense, tells them is worth
questioning. (*Beat.*) It is our hope that the *Leftist Review*
can become that forum for this questioning, for discussing
the changes as they occur – with total freedom and an
open mind. I can think of no greater political use. Or
moral use. Or intellectual or artistic use of a magazine.
(*Pause.*) So now – continuing to imagine ourselves as
Jews, we hear the Party claim to be the standard bearer for
anti-fascism in the world. (*Beat.*) The best hope for all
Jews against Hitler. This is what Stalin claims to be.
(*Beat.*) It's a view of the world, we believe, at least worth
discussing, questioning.

(*Long pause.* EDWARD *sits down.* ELINOR *suddenly turns her
head towards the porch door.*)

ELINOR: I thought I heard something.

(*Short pause.*)

MARIANNE: (*To* EDWARD) The last time you gave that speech
you needed to use notes.

EDWARD: I've been practising.

MARIANNE: It shows. (*Beat.*) But still – so what does Gene
care? Why should he – he's not a Jew?

ELINOR: By the way, are you sure?

EDWARD: 'Hopkins'?

ELINOR: So what the hell, at least it can't hurt.

MARIANNE: It could if he hates Jews.

EDWARD: He doesn't hate Jews. Gene Hopkins doesn't hate Jews, Marianne.

(*Short pause.*)

ELINOR: Then fine. It can't hurt. So – it's my turn. (*Beat.*) I think if I just get very emotional at this point. Ideological priorities can be questioned by other things than being Jewish. You just have to look around New York and see what is happening to a society. A civilization. (*Beat.*) The breadlines. Slums. Hunger. Pain. The children. (*Beat.*) The children. I could get really really emotional about what is happening to so many children. If I let myself go, I could be –

(*Suddenly noise off.*)

EDWARD: What's that?

(*He goes to the porch door and opens it.*)

MARIANNE: What is it?

(*She hurries after him.*)

EDWARD: It's Gene. (*Calls*:) Gene!! (*Beat.*) He's taking off in his seaplane.

(*He goes out.* MARIANNE *follows.*)

ELINOR: Gene? Where's he going?

(ELINOR *follows. Pause.*)

1986. The setting is unchanged. The OLDER ELINOR *enters with* PETER *from the kitchen.*

ELINOR: (*Entering*) You see I knew right where the matches were. Same drawer as three years ago. Old people get into such ruts, Peter. It's so tiresome. (*Hands him the matches.*) Here, you do it. Or do you want me?

PETER: I can do it if you like.

(*Short pause. He begins to light a couple of the kerosene lamps.*)

ELINOR: Of course, a man of your talents – motorboat driver, bedmaker, lawyer. (*Goes back to the chair. Short pause.*) Anything else you can't find – (*She sits. Pause.*) Perhaps we should disturb them. (*Nods in the direction of the bedroom*.) Remind them that we're here. Maybe they forgot. It's been – (*Looks at her watch*.) On second thought better not, what if they're fooling around in there?

PETER: Right.

ELINOR: You think they're fooling around in there?

PETER: No. (*Beat*.) I heard them talking. I heard their voices.

ELINOR: I heard nothing.

PETER: Anything else you want me to do? Otherwise I'll go back and –

ELINOR: (*Ignoring him*) What were we just talking about? Old people. Right. It seems I've been spending so much more of my time with old people recently. (*Beat*.) These past few years. Perhaps it's my calling. Like Florence Nightingale among the sick. Elinor Blair among the old and decrepit. Take a biscuit with you. Eat while you cook. I always did. (*Holds up the tray*.) Here.

(PETER *takes a biscuit*.)

PETER: Thank you.

(*He starts to go to the kitchen*.)

ELINOR: I bought them for her. They're English. She'll never eat them though. She'll think they're poisoned.

(PETER *smiles*.)

But tell me, Peter, why would I poison her when she's already dying?

(PETER *grimaces*.)

Why would I, Peter?

PETER: I don't know. Excuse me.

(*He goes into the kitchen. Short pause*.)

ELINOR: (*Calls*) It was a joke! I was making a joke. (*Beat*.) It's always the young who can't take a joke. The young and the lawyers. (*Beat*.) Peter, what's the difference between a dead snake on the highway and a dead lawyer on the highway? (*Beat*.) In front of the dead snake there are skid marks. (*Pause. In a loud voice*) My godson told me that. He learned it at his school. Harvard Law School. They take such jokes as compliments there.

(*Long pause*.)

Eddie ate a biscuit. (*Beat*.) He'd love it if I poisoned him.

21

His posthumous literary reputation would be made.
(*Pause. To herself*) Abandoned, I could have stayed home
and felt abandoned.

SCENE 5

Projection: 8.05 p.m.
1937. Setting the same, though with a few more gaslights lit.
MARIANNE *and* ELINOR *sit on the couch;* EDWARD *stands behind
them.* THERESE, *an attractive and well-dressed woman in her late
twenties, stands at the kitchen door, stirring something in a bowl.
She wears an apron.*

THERESE: Lucky I happened by with all this food. Gene's left
    nothing in the ice-box.
MARIANNE: We would have managed.
EDWARD: Thank you for sharing with us. I hope we aren't –
THERESE: Hey, it's nice to be with people. There's no one at
    my place. (*Beat.*) So I'm lucky too. I'll start getting the
    plates.
ELINOR: Let me –
THERESE: No. No. Gene wouldn't hear of it. You're his
    guests.
MARIANNE: And you?
THERESE: I'm a friend. I drop by all the time. Excuse me.
    (*She goes into the kitchen. Short pause.*)
EDWARD: Who is she?
ELINOR: Thérèse, she said.
EDWARD: I don't mean her name.
ELINOR: (*Shrugs.*) A friend of Gene's? I guess she lives around
    here. (*Beat.*) She's certainly attractive, isn't she?
MARIANNE: You think so? I don't think she's attractive.
    Eddie, do you think she's attractive?
EDWARD: No. (*Beat.*) Not really. Not that attractive. (*Beat.*)
    It's the clothes that make her seem attractive.
THERESE: (*Entering with plates*) The one thing you could do is
    get me that drink.

22

EDWARD: Sorry. I forgot. (*Goes to the bar.*) Manhattan, wasn't it?

THERESE: Anything.

(*Pause.* THERESE *puts each plate down.*)

I forgot to ask if you all like chops?

(*They all nod.*)

Good. That's a relief. (*Beat.*) I believe Gene keeps the silverware – (*Goes to a drawer and opens it.*) I was right. (*She takes out silverware.*)

ELINOR: Are you sure we couldn't –

THERESE: Absolutely not. Gene's going to be sick when he realizes he's abandoned you. He'd be mortified as well if he also heard you set your own table. (*Starts to set the table. Stops.*) Some candles would be nice. (*Starts to go into the kitchen. Stops. To* MARIANNE *and* ELINOR) You two aren't in the theatre by any chance?

ELINOR: Us? No. No.

MARIANNE: Why do you ask?

THERESE: It's your faces. They're so – interesting. Beautiful really, if you don't mind my saying so.

ELINOR: Thank you.

THERESE: (*Moving towards the kitchen*) Gene has a lot of friends in the theatre.

EDWARD: And me? Do I look like I'm in the theatre?

THERESE: No. (*Beat. As she leaves*) Not at all. Not a bit. (*Pause.*)

(*Off*) You can bring that drink in here, if you don't mind.

EDWARD: Oh, sorry.

(*He takes the drink into the kitchen. Short pause.*)

ELINOR: (*Without looking at* MARIANNE) She's wearing a wedding ring.

MARIANNE: (*Without looking at* ELINOR) A diamond and a band. Two rings.

ELINOR: So she's married?

(MARIANNE *shrugs.*)

Her husband's not up here. She said no one was up here. (*Beat.*) She seems nice.

MARIANNE: When you are rich you can afford to seem nice.

23

(*Beat.*) And besides, it's cheap.

ELINOR: Come on, what has she done?

MARIANNE: It's what she is, Elinor. There were girls like her everywhere at Smith.

ELINOR: Rich girls?

MARIANNE: Rich girls like her. They think about nothing. They care about nothing really. (*Beat.*) I mean, she is so transparent. I will bet you anything she is having an affair with Gene. And in fact expected to see Gene here tonight – alone. That's the reason for all the food.

ELINOR: Maybe. Maybe not.

MARIANNE: And when she saw us – we surprised her. You have to admit that – she was not expecting us – well, all this politeness, it's to disguise what we in fact walked in on. (*Beat.*) Elinor, use your eyes, for God's sake.

ELINOR: So? What if you're right? It's none of our business.

MARIANNE: That's just my point. I just don't like rich people dragging me into their fickle frivolous lives.
(*Laughter from the kitchen. Short pause.*)
And as for Eddie, I cannot begin to describe my disappointment in him. First it was Gene. Now this DAR bitch.

ELINOR: I wouldn't think the name Thérèse was exactly –

MARIANNE: Has he no pride? That's what I would like to know.

ELINOR: He's talking to her in the kitchen. What's he doing?

MARIANNE: He's attracted to her. You can see that, can't you. He pretty much said as much.

ELINOR: She's an attractive –

MARIANNE: You too?! I can't even talk to you too.

ELINOR: You can talk –

MARIANNE: All of you – go to hell! Forget it! (*Gets up.*) Forget I'm even here!

ELINOR: Marianne!

MARIANNE: I'm going to my cabin for the night. Have fun. Enjoy yourself. As for me, I think the dinner conversation alone would drive me to murder.
(*She goes out of the porch door. Pause. Laughter from the kitchen.*)

24

EDWARD: (*Entering with* THERESE; *they carry candles*)
Incredible. Let them hear this. Thérèse has been these
last – how many months?
THERESE: Five. I think we should put them all (*The candles*) on
the table.
EDWARD: Five months. In Spain.
ELINOR: Spain?
EDWARD: Two on each side, I think.
(*They put the candles down.*)
ELINOR: Thérèse, you've been in Spain?
EDWARD: (*Suddenly noticing*) Where's Marianne?
ELINOR: She went to her cabin.
THERESE: Will she be long? The dinner's nearly –
ELINOR: I don't think we should wait.
(*Pause.*)
THERESE: (*To* EDWARD) I hope it wasn't something I –
EDWARD: No. If you knew Marianne better you'd understand
it has nothing to do with you.
ELINOR: Eddie, what does that mean?
THERESE: Sit down, dear, I'll set the table (*Beat.*) Eddie, I
seem to have misplaced my drink.
EDWARD: In the kitchen. I'll be right back.
(*He goes into the kitchen.*)
THERESE: (*To* ELINOR) She's a very striking woman, your
friend, Marianne. Eyes like flames. Very striking.
EDWARD: (*Entering with the drink*) Here it is.
THERESE: Thank you. (*Takes the glass and drinks it down.*)
Could I have another please? (*Beat.*) American liquor
tastes like water to me after Spain.
(EDWARD, *rather stunned, takes the glass and goes to the bar
to pour another.*)
ELINOR: What exactly were you doing in Spain?
EDWARD: She was in an actual militia.
THERESE: (*Setting the silverware*) There was a woman's militia.
EDWARD: With guns and cannons. They actually give the
women guns.
ELINOR: I knew that.
THERESE: You haven't been to Spain?

ELINOR: I was thinking of going last year.

THERESE: Take it from me, when you do go, go with as few expectations as possible. That's what I did and brother did it help. He seems not to have enough soup spoons. (*She goes to the silverware drawer.*)

ELINOR: Excuse me, I think Marianne would be very very interested in hearing this. About Spain. Just a minute. (*She has gone to the porch door and opened it.*)
(*Calls:*) Marianne!!!

EDWARD: Think of the courage it must have taken –

THERESE: Not courage.
(*He holds out her drink.*)
Thank you. Put it on the table. (*Beat.*) I don't know what it was, but I don't think it had anything to do with courage. Curiosity maybe. I simply wanted to experience this great thing happening. Now where would he keep the napkins?
(*She opens a cabinet.*)

ELINOR: And your husband, Thérèse?
(*She looks up.*)
I noticed the rings . . . (*Beat.*) Didn't he try to –

THERESE: Talk me out of going? (*Takes out napkins and goes to the table.*) Actually – no. But don't be too surprised by that. Harvey and I have been having sort of a hard time of it lately.

EDWARD: I'm sorry.

THERESE: Don't be.
(*Short pause.*)

ELINOR: He's not up –?

THERESE: Here? No.(*Beat.*) Not this week.

ELINOR: Oh.

THERESE: It's all my fault really. I never should have introduced him to my friend, Josie. See – she was my friend first. I met her first. (*Beat.*) Beautiful girl. We'd spent the whole summer camping together in Montana. The sky out there. It's everything they say it is. It's so romantic. (*Beat.*) You and your friend, Marianne, should try camping out there sometime.

26

ELINOR: Yeh.

THERESE: Josie and I had met in a bar in Chicago. I was
changing trains. I mean, who knew that this girl with
those big brown eyes could also type? (*Smiles to herself.*) I
don't know how it happened, but somehow Harvey made
her his secretary. She travels with him all the time now.
Sometimes I go along too – but I find that sort of thing
really confusing. Anyway, instead of trying to argue me
out of it, Harvey got me a press card from *Time Life*. He
said that was something he could do for me. So off I went
to Spain. (*Short pause.*) I guess what it comes down to is he
called my bluff. (*Short pause.*) On the other hand I've
often wondered if Harvey didn't see it as a plus – my being
over there fighting the fascists. When you're dealing with
defence contracts all the time like he is, having some tie to
someone with a belief, well, it helps create the illusion that
there is more to you than just greed. I don't know. (*Drinks
down her drink.*) One more and then let's open the wine.
(EDWARD *takes her glass.* MARIANNE *is at the porch door
looking in. She holds a lantern.*)

THERESE: What are you three, still in college or what?

MARIANNE: No.
(EDWARD *and* ELINOR *turn to her, seeing her there for the
first time.*)
No, we're not in –

THERESE: (*Not listening*) Speaking of wine. Do you know how
they open wine bottles in Spain? Not all bottles. I only
saw this once, but – (*Beat.*) They take a dog. I saw them
do this with a collie. Part collie. And they take the dog's
penis and tape it to the top of the bottle and then they start
rubbing its balls and the idea, see, is that the erection will
push in the cork. (*Laughs to herself.*) Never saw it work.
(*Beat.*) There are things happening in Spain that you or I
never even imagined.
(EDWARD *hands her her drink.*)
Thank you. We should be ready in just a few minutes.
(*Throughout the rest of the scene* THERESE *goes back and
forth from the kitchen bringing out dishes, glasses, etc.*)

There was a particular *cabo* – that's corporal. She was the one who convinced me to join the woman's militia. A huge woman. She was Russian. (*Beat.*) Burgundy OK with everyone? (*Beat.*) And she had us – the women – out chopping wood in the forest one morning. Except for these two English comrades who were going to stand guard between us and the line, we all had set down our rifles so we could chop. We needed the wood. (*Beat.*) It gets pretty damn cold in Spain in January. And now it is bitter cold. (*Beat.*) Suddenly we see this man come through the woods. We all stop and freeze. The two with their guns – the English girls from Manchester – point them. Then, this man, unaware that here are forty or so young women with axes a few yards away from him, he pulls down his pants and squats. (*Beat.*) Well, the Russian comrade – the *cabo* – she gestures for none of us to move, and she silently picks up her gun, and then – she screams: 'Stand up!' (*Beat.*) In Spanish. (*Beat.*) The man stands up, with his pants now – And you see his face as he sees himself standing there, and we are a crowd of women not only with rifles but also with these very sharp axes. (*Laughs to herself as she continues to serve the meal.*) I think he was an anarchist actually. POUM most likely. You should have seen his boots – nothing really left of them. Also he had a lot of body hair – so he looked like a farmer, not a fascist. So – POUM. Anyway, the *cabo*, she goes up to him and without so much as hesitating – (*Smiles to herself.*) She grabs ahold of his penis and gives it a huge tug. (*Pours the soup.*) And he's on the ground now and she says – 'I wanted to ring your bell.' (*Laughs to herself.*) In Spanish she says this. 'Ring your bell.' (*Beat.*) That's an expression we had, there was a song – it's a pun really. (*Beat.*) It was very funny. (*Beat.*) That's war for you. (*Beat.*) That and body lice. (*Beat.*) For some reason international proletarian solidarity and body lice will be forever linked in my mind. (*Beat.*) Dinner is served. Eddie, do you want to open the wine?

Projection: 8.50 p.m.
1986. Setting the same. EDWARD, ELINOR *and* PETER *are at the
table in the late stages of eating dinner. A fourth place is also set.
As they eat* EDWARD *reads a newspaper which he holds next to his
plate. Flowers on the table. Pause.*

ELINOR: She's had a very long nap. (*Beat.*) She's been in there
all afternoon. (*Beat.*) Perhaps someone should . . .
(PETER *begins to stand up.*)
I didn't mean you, Peter. (*Beat.*) You can't do everything
in this house.
(PETER *sits back down.*)
When George was ill I tried to do everything. I felt I owed
it to George. He was my husband. (*Beat.*) We were
married. I cared about him. (*Beat.*) If he'd taken such a
long nap . . . (*Short pause.*) Delicious soup, Peter.
PETER: Thank you, Elinor.
(*Pause.*)
ELINOR: (*To* EDWARD) Anything in the paper? I am very glad
to see you enjoying the paper. I brought it so you would
enjoy it. (*Short pause.*) You're welcome, Eddie. (*Beat.*)
Actually, Peter, I brought it for me to read on the train.
And then I just kept it. At the last minute I remembered
Eddie and I kept it. (*Beat.*) He was simply a last second's
thought. (*Eats.*) I don't eat potato skins. Did you know
that's where the vitamins are? In the skins. We'll put
them in the compost. Eddie, Peter tells me he didn't even
know you kept a compost.
PETER: I –
ELINOR: That compost has been there forever, Eddie. Think
of what has been thrown out. Think of what has been –
(*Beat.*) lost.
(EDWARD *looks up from his newspaper. Then takes a sip from
his drink.*)
Peter, do you play golf?
PETER: Yes, I do.

(*Pause.*)

ELINOR: That's it. I only had that one question.

(EDWARD *laughs under his breath.* ELINOR *smiles, realizing she is slowly getting* EDWARD's *attention.*)

My biggest fear, Peter, in coming here – and did I have fears – do I – I never thought of myself as courageous before, but now, sitting here – (*Laughs to herself.*) What was I saying?

PETER: Your biggest fear about coming here.

ELINOR: What's my biggest fear? (*Beat.*) Eddie. I hoped he wouldn't blame me. Marianne – really, what do I care about what she thinks?

PETER: But I thought Marianne was your closest friend.

ELINOR: Young man, I am not on a witness stand so I would appreciate it if you would not speak to me in that tone of voice

PETER: But –

ELINOR: And I am only going to tell you once.

PETER: Sorry. (*Beat.*) I'm very sorry. (*Short pause.*)

ELINOR: (*Smiling*) Eddie, look at him, he believed me.

(*She laughs.* EDWARD *tries not to laugh but does.*)

When you're ready, Peter, you can take my plate. I've had all I can take.

(*Short pause. She gets up and goes to the couch.*)

PETER: I think I'm finished as well.

(*He stands, begins to collect plates.*)

Eddie?

EDWARD: No.

(PETER *takes dishes into the kitchen.*)

ELINOR: The flowers are lovely. Daffodils have always been a favourite of mine, as you know only too well. (*Beat.*) The ones in my cabin are even lovelier.

(*Pause.* PETER *comes out and picks up the rest of the plates, except for* EDWARD's.)

PETER: (*Leaving*) I'll do the dishes.

(*Beat. He goes.*)

ELINOR: What a strange experience it is to walk into a cabin and know that you were expected by the flowers on the dresser. (*Beat.*) I almost felt hurt.

(EDWARD *looks up.*)
Being known like that. Sometimes such gestures are
touching – they mean: be comfortable, you are among
friends. (*Beat.*) Other times, they mean – we know who you
are, we know everything, you are among friends.
(EDWARD *turns a page of the newspaper.*)
You were always a man with a newspaper. That's how I
remember you. You were always interested in things. What
interests you now? These days. (*Beat.*) This interest in
things is what always made you so –

EDWARD: I'm getting interested in writing my memoirs, Elinor.
(*He eats.*)

ELINOR: Good for you.

EDWARD: That doesn't frighten you?

ELINOR: No. (*Beat.*) Why should it?

EDWARD: Perhaps you'd give me a decent advance.

ELINOR: I don't acquire books any more, Eddie. Not since the
Brits bought –

EDWARD: I'd take half the advance Dorothy Gilbert got.

ELINOR: I know what people say but I had nothing to do with
the cancellation of Dorothy's book. I don't even know what
she said about me in her book. I wasn't the editor. I wasn't
involved in the decision. (*Beat.*) I don't care what people
say about me. People can say the moon about me. But that's
not me. I don't work like that. (*Short pause.*) Dorothy and
Fred were great friends. (*Beat.*) There were a great many
errors of fact in Dorothy's memoir. The legal department
cancelled the contract. People could have sued. (*Beat.*)
With cause.

EDWARD: (*Continuing to eat*) It was only a thought. I simply
wanted you to know that I can be bought off. With the right
advance our three years of marriage will be erased from
time.

ELINOR: I would not want to see those years erased, Eddie.
Believe me. I say that with all my heart.
(*With tears in her eyes she goes to him and hugs him from
behind. He continues to eat. She stops. She goes back to the
couch.*)

I had no idea you were looking for another publisher. What's Robert done? You've been with him for years and years. (*Beat*.) I talked to Robert just this week. He thinks Marianne's lawsuit is pure garbage. There are so many people on my side. If I were the one dying I wouldn't want to look so foolish. (*Pause*.) What's so bad about what I said about her? I hardly mentioned her. I talked about her politics – not so much about her, Eddie. (*Beat*.) The fact that she takes everything so personally – I do not see this as my problem. If there is any point I wish to make while I'm here, it is this. (*Beat*.) I do not think this is my –
(*A thud off. Short pause. Then a bell.* PETER *enters from the kitchen, looks at* EDWARD *who doesn't move.* PETER *then goes down the hall. After a moment, he comes back.*)

PETER: She fell off the bed (*Beat*.) She won't let me pick her up.

EDWARD: No. She wouldn't.
(EDWARD *gets up and goes down the hall. Short pause.*)

ELINOR: (*Without looking at* PETER) With something like that, it's not the lungs but the brain that's going to kill her. (*Beat*.) That's what happened to George.
(PETER *nods.*)
If it is the lungs that kills her, it'll be very slow and very long.
(*Pause.* PETER *nods and goes back into the kitchen.* ELINOR *sits on the couch.* EDWARD *returns. He sits at the table.*)

EDWARD: In my memoirs –
(*He gets up and goes to the bar and pours himself a large drink. As he does this:*)
Remind me to change the sheets in there before I go to bed. They need changing now. Sometimes I forget. By the time I get to bed I often have forgotten everything. Sometimes I don't even know where I am. Who I am with.
(*He goes back and sits at the table. As he eats:*)
Back in the city I have a closet full of pornography. Floor to ceiling of pornography. (*Beat*.) The *New York Review of Books* – of all people – wanted me to do an essay on

32

pornography. It was going to become a book. The people
there helped me collect the stuff. I had these nice assistant
editors take me around to buy the stuff. That was the
most fun. (*Short pause.*) I would open a book – like this
and show them – show the kids. The boys were even more
embarrassed than the girls. I thought we had lived
through a sexual revolution. (*Beat.*) A closet full – all
bought by the staff of the *New York Review of Books*. I
would put that into my memoirs. (*Beat.*) Never got
around to writing the piece, Elinor. Kept getting caught
up in the research. (*Laughs to himself.*) Whenever I feel old
I start doing more research. (*Laughs.*) When Marianne
and I finally bought this place and stopped visiting –
(*Nods towards* ELINOR.) It wasn't that long ago when you
think about it. Five years maybe? No more than five
years. I remember we closed and Marianne and I – we
went swimming in the lake. Naked. Why not? It's private.
(*Beat.*) Even last year. Once or twice. Those three or four
years. (*Beat.*) Before she started getting dizzy. They said
it was her ulcer acting up. Or another ulcer. So she
stopped drinking. (*Beat.*) It wasn't an ulcer. I had stopped
drinking with her. (*Beat.*) But then it wasn't an ulcer.
(*Short pause.*) You'd think the doctors would have known
better. Don't they deal with this all the time? (*Short
pause.*) Maybe seven months ago we could have gone
swimming naked. She has some body. (*Beat.*) Let me tell
you, Elinor, she's got a lot better body than you do.
(ELINOR *smiles, trying not to cry.*)
What a body. If she hadn't drunk – what an amazing
body. But still – even with – We could have gone
swimming just months ago, except it would have been too
cold. (*Beat.*) But in principle. (*Beat.*) And now it is
definitely warm enough.
(ELINOR *has walked over to* EDWARD, *and again with tears
in her eyes she puts her arms around him, hugs him. He nestles
his head into her shoulder. She rubs his head. This lasts a
while, then he turns, putting his mouth to her neck, and bites.*)
ELINOR: Ow! (*Beat.*) What did you bite me for?

EDWARD: (*Staring at her, calmly*) I thought you liked that. I
    remember you always liking that.
    (*They stare at each other.* PETER *enters.*)
PETER: I could put on some coffee. Or is it too late?

SCENE 7

Projection: Night.
1937 and *1986. Setting the same.*
1937: the OLDER MARIANNE *sits at the table, eating her dinner.*
1986: the YOUNGER MARIANNE *and the* YOUNGER ELINOR *sit on
the couch and chair, playing two-handed bridge.*
OLDER MARIANNE *laughs to herself. Pause.*

YOUNGER ELINOR: What's trump again?
YOUNGER MARIANNE: Clubs. (*Beat.*) Spades. Two spades.
    (*Short pause.*)
YOUNGER ELINOR: It'll be fun.
YOUNGER MARIANNE: We don't know who's going to be there.
YOUNGER ELINOR: If her guests are half as interesting as she
is – She didn't have to invite us.
YOUNGER MARIANNE: She has a rich husband. What's three
    more for brunch?
    (*Short pause.*)
YOUNGER ELINOR: He's taking a long time helping her to her
    boat.
YOUNGER MARIANNE: Just because a woman has a big mouth
    and is willing to say anything – even very personal things,
    pathetic things in my mind – to strangers, this makes her
    an interesting person. (*Laughs.*) You and Eddie
    disappoint me so much sometimes.
    (OLDER MARIANNE *laughs lightly to herself.*)
YOUNGER ELINOR: How many cards do you have? (MARIANNE
    shows her.) Then it is still my play. (*Pause. She plays.*) She
    is very attractive, you have to admit.
YOUNGER MARIANNE: She's nearly thirty. It's at thirty that
    women reach the absolute peak of their beauty.

34

YOUNGER ELINOR: (*Seriously*) I thought it was much younger.
   (OLDER MARIANNE *suddenly laughs out loud*. OLDER
   EDWARD *enters from the porch*.)
OLDER EDWARD: She was still reading. That's what the light was
   for. (*Beat*.) She's fine. She said she was so tired she was afraid
   she couldn't sleep. (*Beat*.) What were you laughing about?
   Just now. (*Short pause*.) When I came in you were laughing.
OLDER MARIANNE: I was thinking.
   (*Short pause*.)
OLDER EDWARD: I'm going to get ready for bed.
OLDER MARIANNE: So soon? We usually have a drink together
   before you go to bed.
OLDER EDWARD: I'll change the sheets and come back out.
   (*Starts to go*. *Stops*.) I told her it was your idea to check on
   her. That you were the one concerned. She said she didn't
   believe that.
   (*Short pause*.)
OLDER MARIANNE: I was concerned – about the lamp battery.
   They're expensive.
   (*He smiles. Goes to her and kisses her. She kisses him back. He
   begins to kiss her neck, then bites her*.)
   Ow.
   (*He pulls back*.)
   That was nice. (*Beat*.) You're very sexy.
   (*He smiles and goes down the hallway. She continues to eat*.)
YOUNGER MARIANNE: Listen.
YOUNGER ELINOR: What is it? (*Beat*.) A bird.
YOUNGER MARIANNE: A loon. I'm sure it must be a loon.
   (*They listen*.)
YOUNGER ELINOR: That's a lonely sound. Makes you cry.
YOUNGER MARIANNE: Everything makes you cry, Elinor.
   (YOUNGER ELINOR *smiles*. YOUNGER EDWARD *comes in
   from the porch*.)
YOUNGER EDWARD: Well, she's off. (*Beat*.) Anyone else want a
   drink? (*They say nothing. He goes to bar*.) She'll pick us up at
   eleven thirty. (*Short pause*.) I had a good time tonight and I
   am not going to say I didn't. (*Short pause*.) Thérèse may be
   eccentric, but eccentric people have their place in the world.

YOUNGER MARIANNE: (*Ignoring him, almost interrupting*)
Eddie, what are our plans, if I may ask?
YOUNGER EDWARD: Tomorrow, Thérèse will pick us up –
YOUNGER MARIANNE: How long do we stay?!
(*Short pause.*)
YOUNGER EDWARD: We can go whenever you want.
YOUNGER MARIANNE: I am not the one who brought us here
and I am not going to be the one who decides that we go.
(*Pause.*)
YOUNGER EDWARD: Elinor?
(ELINOR *shrugs. Pause.*)
How long can Gene be gone for? (*Beat.*) He's left us the
boat. So we can go whenever we want.
(*Pause. The younger women continue to play cards. The*
OLDER MARIANNE *eats.* YOUNGER EDWARD *sips his drink.*)
(*Finally*) We were out by her boat talking, and suddenly
she she stops and asks – which of you two did I sleep with.
(*Short pause.*)
YOUNGER ELINOR: She did?
YOUNGER EDWARD: Yeh.
YOUNGER MARIANNE: What did you say?
(EDWARD *shrugs. Short pause.*)
YOUNGER EDWARD: We're colleagues. We work together.
YOUNGER MARIANNE: Right. (*Pause.*) You know I'm not
surprised she asked him that.
YOUNGER ELINOR: Why?
YOUNGER MARIANNE: Some people aren't happy unless they
can drag everything down to the personal.
(*Beat. And then suddenly the* OLDER MARIANNE *starts to
laugh, as if she has heard the funniest joke in the world.*)

ACT TWO

SCENE 8

Projection: THE NEXT DAY – 8.15 a.m.
The lawn which overlooks the beach and lake. To one side (unseen)
the cabins, to the other (also unseen) the main house. Outdoor
wooden chairs, including two reclining chairs; side tables, a larger
table, etc. 1986: The OLDER MARIANNE *sits; she wears a sun hat;*
she is reading Elinor's book.
1937: YOUNGER EDWARD, MARIANNE *and* ELINOR *sit, having*
coffee. MARIANNE *has a robe on,* ELINOR *and* EDWARD *have*
towels around themselves. Pause. YOUNGER ELINOR *puts back her*
head and closes her eyes.

ELINOR: Mmmm. The sun does feel good.
EDWARD: Doesn't it? (*Beat.*) Nice after a swim.
ELINOR: Yes. Very nice.
    (*Short pause.*)
MARIANNE: You know, Elinor, you were right.
ELINOR: (*Without opening her eyes*) I know.
MARIANNE: You don't even know what I was going to say.
    (*Beat.*) I mean, about swimming like this. (*Beat.*) Without
    suits on.
ELINOR: (*Still with eyes closed*) I knew what you were going to
    say.
MARIANNE: It's great. It really is.
ELINOR: I know. (*Opens her eyes, and picks up her sun lotion and*
    begins to put some on her shoulders.) I can hardly stand to put
    a suit on any more. It changes the whole thing.
EDWARD: I agree (*Smiles.*) But I wouldn't want to do it with
    someone like Thérèse. She'd probably try to – 'ring my bell'.
    (*He laughs at his joke. No one else does.*)
ELINOR: (*Ignoring* EDWARD) There is really something very
    pure about it.
EDWARD: (*Trying to get back into the conversation*) Oh, I agree.
    Very pure.

37

(*Beat.*)

ELINOR: After all, *we* are the ones who put the clothes on. We weren't exactly born that way.

(*Short pause.*)

MARIANNE: (*To* ELINOR) Who do you usually go – swimming with?

ELINOR: Whomever.

MARIANNE: Really?

ELINOR: Does it matter? Sometimes I just go by myself. If there's someone else there – You just ignore them. In a way it's a very private thing. (*She finishes with the sun lotion and begins to pour herself more coffee.*) More coffee? (*The others shake their heads. Pause.*)

MARIANNE: It is pure. That is the word for it, isn't it?

ELINOR: That's not to say there isn't a sensuality about it.

MARIANNE: I didn't mean –

EDWARD: Yes, there's definitely that.

ELINOR: Drifting there. Stretching out. I like to just float. It's very comforting I've found. (*Beat.*) Very stimulating. (EDWARD *nods but says nothing. He pours himself some coffee.*)

MARIANNE: I wouldn't call it sexual –

ELINOR: No, no, sensual. I chose the word very carefully. There's a huge difference between –

MARIANNE: Of course.

(*Beat.*)

ELINOR: Sensual has a lot more to do with than just one's sex parts.

EDWARD: Though there's some of that –

ELINOR: I don't think so. (*Beat. To* MARIANNE) What do you think?

MARIANNE: I don't know.

ELINOR: What it essentially has to do with is – being free. Being without encumbrances. Having your body very much alive, touching everything. But then, maybe it's not the same for a man.

EDWARD: No, it's wonderful.

ELINOR: The sense of being unshackled, I mean.

EDWARD: Yes, it's very freeing.

ELINOR: You'd do it again?

EDWARD: Of course.

ELINOR: (*To* MARIANNE) I'm still not sure if the pleasure's the same for him. (*To* EDWARD) Would you do it alone? Was there this wonderfully sensual pleasure of just being naked in the water, or was the real thrill having a couple of naked women floating right near you?

EDWARD: I – (*Beat.*) I'd do it alone. I would. I enjoyed it. What do you want me to say?

(ELINOR *smiles and then laughs,* MARIANNE *laughs as well; very much excluding* EDWARD *from their joke. Both women close their eyes and lean back. Long pause.*)

(*Finally*) Have you read that Henry Miller book?

ELINOR: (*With eyes closed*) Who? What book?

MARIANNE: I know what you mean.

EDWARD: (*To* ELINOR) I'll show it to you. You can't buy it. (*Beat.*) A friend sent it from Paris. If they'd opened it at customs –

MARIANNE: It wouldn't have been your fault.

EDWARD: They'd have taken it. I could have been fined.

MARIANNE: What if you didn't even know what it was? What if I sent you something that I wasn't supposed to and you didn't even know what it was? They couldn't fine you.

EDWARD: I knew what it was! I asked my friend to send it. (*Beat.*) I was taking a big chance. (*Short pause.*) Incredibly graphic. But not at all sensual.

ELINOR: Doesn't sound –

EDWARD: Not at all erotic.

ELINOR: You're not equating sensual with erotic – ?

MARIANNE: I don't think he meant –

EDWARD: I wasn't equating anything. All I said was it wasn't sensual *and* it wasn't erotic.

ELINOR: Define what you mean by 'erotic'.

EDWARD: It means – (*Beat.*) Something that is erotic, it stimulates. Causes physical stimulation. Verifiable physical stimulation.

ELINOR: That's good. That's a very good definition.

MARIANNE: It is.

    (*Pause.*)

EDWARD: Miller goes way overboard. Actually, by the end it's
    become quite political; its statement becomes really a
    political statement. I don't think intentionally. But you
    can't help to see these people as decadent. As if nothing
    exists but their . . .

MARIANNE: Cocks?

    (ELINOR *looks at* MARIANNE.)

EDWARD: Yeh. Right. Their 'cocks', as you say.

MARIANNE: You should review it. Sounds like something
    worth bringing up. Not the book. What you have to say
    about the book.

EDWARD: I was thinking of doing that. (*Beat.*) That's why I
    took the chance and had my friend send me a copy.
    (*Pause.*) Whitman's very erotic.

ELINOR: You think so?

EDWARD: Definitely.

ELINOR: What about Joyce?

EDWARD: I don't think of him as –

ELINOR: Have you ever read Molly Bloom out loud? If you
    think Whitman's – (*Getting up*) Wait a minute. I saw a
    copy in the house. Let me get it.

MARIANNE: Elinor –

ELINOR: (*Going into the house*) He's not going to believe this.
    (*She goes. Short pause.*)

MARIANNE: She's read it to me twice.

    (EDWARD *nods. Short pause. She reaches over and picks up*
    Elinor's sun lotion and begins to put a little on her shoulders.)
    You really should do that review of the Henry Miller.
    (*Beat.*) How graphic does he really get?

EDWARD: I'll loan you the book if you want.

MARIANNE: If it's junk –

EDWARD: It's fascinating. To see just how far – How corrupt –
    By the end I think one is just angry at these people, who
    think about nothing but themselves, and as you have so
    succinctly put it – their cocks.

ELINOR: (*Entering with a copy of* Ulysses) I'll just read from the very end. I'll start at random –

MARIANNE: With him how do we know it is at random?

ELINOR: Marianne –

MARIANNE: I was joking. (*To* EDWARD) Give me Dreiser any day.

ELINOR: Just the last – Here.

(*She stays standing and begins to read; occasionally as she reads she has to fix her towel to keep it up.*)

'. . . where I was a Flower of the mountain yes when I put the rose in my hair like the Andalusian girls used or shall I wear a red yes and how he kissed me under the Moorish wall and I thought well as well him as another and then I asked him with my eyes to ask again yes and then he asked me would I yes to say yes my mountain flower and first I put my arms around him yes and drew him down to me so he could feel my breasts all perfume yes and his heart was going like mad and yes I said yes I will Yes.' (*She closes the book. Pause.*) It's the rhythm with the yesses –

EDWARD: It's very clever. You're right, you need to hear it out loud.

ELINOR: You get some of it just reading –

EDWARD: But I'm sure nothing like –

ELINOR: No. (*Beat.*) I diagrammed the whole last three pages for a paper.

EDWARD: May I – ?

(*She hands him the book. He opens it to the last page.*)

(*After a moment*) Look.

ELINOR: What?

(*She goes to look.*)

EDWARD: He capitalizes the very last 'Yes'.

(*She looks. He holds up the book for* MARIANNE *to see.*)

See? I wonder if anyone's written about that.

SCENE 9

Projection: 9.25 a.m.
The lawn. 1986. The OLDER MARIANNE, *as in the previous scene,*

41

sits; she is reading Elinor's book. The OLDER EDWARD *slowly enters from the direction of the cabins. Short pause. Suddenly the* OLDER MARIANNE *slams the book shut, sighs and looks up.*

EDWARD: Getting ourselves pumped up for the fight? (*Beat.*) You've been out here for a while now. That much sun isn't –

MARIANNE: Is it time yet? (*Beat.*) I hope she doesn't chicken out and try to settle. Though that would be just like her, wouldn't it?

EDWARD: No.

MARIANNE: No guts, that woman. (*Holds the book.*) You feel that on every page. You know what really bothers me about this book? It's not what she writes about me. I couldn't give a damn about that. What people want to say about me, let them say it. (*Beat.*) It's like water off my back. (*Beat.*) I mean – really what can you do? (*Laughs.*) No. It's what she's written about you, Eddie, that has me really upset. To me – that is unconscionable. Even at our age we can still be shocked by how low people will stoop. (*Short pause.*) Actually I'm a little surprised you've not been more upset with her than you are. (*Beat.*) But you always did hide your feelings pretty well. (*Beat.*) You're hiding your feelings pretty well now, Eddie.

EDWARD: I'm not in the index. I'm never named in the whole –

MARIANNE: But anyone who knows you, Eddie, knows who you are in this. (*Beat.*) Don't kid yourself. (*Beat.*) To take apart an old friend – an ex-husband. I mean, what could be more cowardly? What could be easier? I'll bet you know things about Elinor that –

EDWARD: Marianne, if I can ignore what's written about me, and you don't care what she wrote about you, then –

MARIANNE: (*Thumbing through the book*) Look at this. Not one word of what I achieved as an educator. Instead, I'm –

EDWARD: They're her memoirs, not yours.

MARIANNE: She's hurt me, Eddie! (*Beat.*) A sick woman like me. Hold my hand.
(*He does.*)

Why don't you tell me that you love me?

EDWARD: I love you.

(PETER *enters from the direction of the cabins*.)

PETER: (*Entering*) I can't get her to change her mind.

MARIANNE: (*To* EDWARD) What?

EDWARD: Elinor doesn't want to leave her cabin. She wants to
have our discussion about her book there.

MARIANNE: But I said I wanted to meet in the main house.
Wasn't she told that?

EDWARD: That's when she said she wanted to meet in *her*
cabin.

(*Short pause*.)

MARIANNE: I can't believe she's that insensitive. So she
expects you to carry me . . .

PETER: She says she's ill too.

(*Beat*.)

EDWARD: She didn't say anything about being ill ten minutes
ago.

PETER: No. (*Beat*.) I think it just came to her talking to me.
(*Pause*.)

MARIANNE: There's no food in that cabin, so we'll just starve
her out. Or better yet – let's call over to the motel,
perhaps there are some people who'd like to rent the cabin
for the night. Pick me up.

EDWARD: Just a –

MARIANNE: Edward, she's made her move, now we have to
make ours. Pick me up!

EDWARD: So what's so wrong with meeting in her cabin?

(*Pause*. MARIANNE *stares at* EDWARD.)

PETER: I'll talk to her again, maybe we can work out a
compromise place to meet.

MARIANNE: How about here on the lawn? (*Beat*.) I'm already
here.

PETER: I think that would be her problem.

(*He starts to go*.)

MARIANNE: Whose side are you on anyway?

PETER: I'm on no one's side, Marianne.

(*He goes*.)

MARIANNE: Did you hear that? He's on no one's side! So what do we pay him for?!

EDWARD: We don't pay him. He's my nephew. He's here on vacation.

(*Pause.*)

MARIANNE: Pick me up, please. I'm getting very hot here.

(*He lifts her up.*)

That stupid woman. (*Short pause.*) How petty can you get? (*Beat. As he carries her off towards the house*) Be careful of your back, Eddie.

(*They go.*)

SCENE 10

Projection: Noon.
The lawn.
1937. YOUNGER EDWARD *sits to one side, reading a newspaper.*
1986. The OLDER ELINOR *and* PETER *stand; she leans against the back of a chair. They have just strolled in. Short pause.*

ELINOR: You're right, Peter. It does feel good to get some air. (*Beat.*) You know I couldn't even get my window closed last night. (*Beat.*) I think it was because of the window that I –

(*She holds her throat.*)

PETER: I'm sorry. I will close it. (*Short pause.*) She was out here. I'm sure they're just inside. Why don't you come in, you haven't had anything to –

ELINOR: I'm taking a stroll. I'll be down by the lake if anyone's interested.

(*She starts to go.*)

PETER: Elinor.

ELINOR: (*Turns back.*) I'm as old as she is! I deserve at least as much respect! (*Beat.*) Tell her I came four hundred miles. I don't see why she can't come one hundred feet.

PETER: She can't walk.

ELINOR: She gets around. When she wants to she gets around.

44

(*Beat.*)
Half my friends won't see me because she's gotten around
to them. (*Short pause.*) You want to stroll with me?

PETER: (*Shakes his head.*) Sorry.

ELINOR: She must pay you a lot.

PETER: Edward's my uncle.

ELINOR: Nepotism? So you're cheap. (*Laughs.*) Can't get your
own clients? Have to rely on the family? (*Beat.*) That's
good to know. (*Beat.*) She was always cheap.
(*She goes off towards the lake.* PETER *hurries off towards the
house.*)

1937. YOUNGER ELINOR *enters from the house with a deck of
cards.* (*They are all dressed to go to Thérèse's.*)

YOUNGER ELINOR: (*Entering*) I found them. They were under
the cushion on the couch. You still want to play?

EDWARD: (*Putting the paper down and standing up*) It's last
week's paper. Where's Marianne?
(*He goes to the table.*)

ELINOR: Going through Gene's bookshelves looking for
something to read.
(*They are at the table now.*)

EDWARD: You can deal. (*Beat.*) And no doubt criticizing
everything Gene has.

ELINOR: (*Shuffling*) Not everything. (*Beat.*) At least I left
before she'd looked through everything. (*Starts to deal.*)
You are sure Thérèse said eleven thirty?

EDWARD: That's what she said.
(*She looks at her watch and shakes her head; then finishes
dealing.* MARIANNE *enters with a book.*)

MARIANNE: Look at this. Jack Wells's book. I didn't even
know it was out.

ELINOR: Neither did I. Let me see.
(*She reaches for the book.*)

MARIANNE: Just a second. It's even inscribed to Gene.

ELINOR: To Gene?

EDWARD: He probably helped him out financially with the
research. Who's Jack Wells?

45

ELINOR: Who's it dedicated to?

MARIANNE: No one. There's no dedication. I thought it'd be for Kitty. (*To* EDWARD) Professor Wells was my adviser; he's the one who suggested that for my thesis on *The Canterbury Tales* I research the wool trade of the fourteenth century.

ELINOR: (*With the book now*) Jack was very to the left.

MARIANNE: You called him 'Jack' too?
  (*Beat.*)

ELINOR: I guess I did.
  (MARIANNE *and* ELINOR *look at each other.*)
  (*To* EDWARD) Whose bid?

EDWARD: Two diamonds.
  (*She puts down her cards and they play. Pause.*)

MARIANNE: (*Having taken the book back*) I used to babysit Miranda. So that's how *I* started calling him 'Jack'. He was the only professor I did that with. It's not so easy calling someone 'professor' when there he'd be puttering around his own house in almost his bare feet.
  (*Pause. She sits down and begins to look through the book.*)
  (*Looking up*) Elinor, why did you call him Jack? He wasn't your adviser.

ELINOR: No.
  (*They play cards. Pause.*)

MARIANNE: You didn't take Chaucer.

ELINOR: (*Without looking up*) I didn't.
  (*Short pause.*)

MARIANNE: (*Closing the book and looking it over*) Handsome binding.

ELINOR: (*While still playing; more to* EDWARD) I'll give him a month before he disowns it. He's disowned everything he's written. He is very hard on himself.

MARIANNE: Is he? (*Beat.*) I didn't know that. I never saw that side of him. We weren't that close.

ELINOR: Right.
  (*Short pause.*)

MARIANNE: I was quite close with Kitty.

ELINOR: Were you?

(*They finish the game.*)
　Are we keeping score?
EDWARD: I don't care.
MARIANNE: Did you know I think I was the first person –
　certainly the first student friend of Kitty's – that she told.
　When she suspected – (*To* EDWARD) She thought Jack
　was seeing someone. (*Beat.*) A student. (*Beat.*) She wasn't
　completely sure, of course. (*Short pause.*) She was a
　fantastic woman. She actually confronted him.
　(EDWARD *is dealing.*)
　He denied it, of course. But, get this, the very next day he
　went out and bought all new underwear.
　(*Beat.*)
ELINOR: What?
EDWARD: Why would he do that?
MARIANNE: I don't know. (*Beat.*) (*To* EDWARD) You don't
　know?
EDWARD: Was there a sale?
MARIANNE: Kitty made it seem very serious.
　(ELINOR *laughs.*)
　What's so funny?
ELINOR: You. (*Laughs again.*) As if making some big point you
　repeat what Kitty told you that the man goes out and buys
　new underwear, but then you don't even know what the
　point's supposed to be!
　(*She laughs.* EDWARD *smiles.*)
MARIANNE: Forget the goddamn underwear!!
EDWARD: (*Turns to calm her*) Marianne –
MARIANNE: Stay out of this. (*Beat.*) I guess what I'm trying to
　ask – as tactfully as I can –
ELINOR: (*Looking through her cards*) What is that?
MARIANNE: If you were the student. (*Beat.*) The student he
　was sleeping with.
ELINOR: I thought Jack denied –
MARIANNE: Kitty didn't believe him. (*Beat.*) I don't believe
　him.
ELINOR: (*To* EDWARD) Let's play.
MARIANNE: Were you?!

47

ELINOR: Why is that your business?

MARIANNE: (*Standing*) Christ! You were!! You were Kitty's friend too!!

ELINOR: Kitty wasn't the innocent victim you think she is.

EDWARD: She isn't?

ELINOR: Keep out of this.

    (*Pause. They play.*)

    I haven't confessed to anything, Marianne.

    (MARIANNE *looks away. Short pause.*)

    He asked me out on a date. OK? What else do you want to know?

MARIANNE: (*Without looking at her*) You went?

ELINOR: I went. What else do you want to know? (*Beat.*) We went to a bar together. He liked to sit *at the bar*. He said it made him feel more – working class. He's a pretty confused man, Marianne. Kitty, he said, would never sit at the bar with him.

MARIANNE: Excuse me –

    (*She starts to leave towards the house.*)

ELINOR: Marianne –

MARIANNE: (*Going*) I just want to put this book back.

    (*She is gone. Pause. They play.*)

ELINOR: Clubs are trumps.

EDWARD: Sorry. Forgot.

    (*He plays a card.*)

ELINOR: (*Playing*) Nothing happened between us. I didn't sleep with Jack Wells.

EDWARD: That's not what you just –

ELINOR: I promise you.

    (*Short pause. They play.* EDWARD *takes a trick.*)

EDWARD: Then why didn't you tell –

ELINOR: I don't know. I don't like being accused.

EDWARD: She only accused you because you wouldn't say you –

ELINOR: I think you should stay out of this.

    (*Short pause.*)

EDWARD: Elinor, tell her. You're arguing about something that didn't even happen.

(MARIANNE *returns*.)

MARIANNE: If you think it's because I'm jealous –

ELINOR: Jealous? About what? That didn't enter my –

MARIANNE: Nothing could be further from the truth. It's
because Kitty was my friend. That's why I am disgusted
at this rich-girl game-playing. Not caring about who the
hell you hurt.

EDWARD: Marianne, Elinor did not –

ELINOR: Be quiet! (*Beat*.) Please, don't give me that holier-
than-thou stuff. I had no more money at school than you
did. Maybe even less.

MARIANNE: I didn't grow up with servants. With chauffeurs. I
was the daughter of a –

ELINOR: Since I was fifteen I've had nothing!

MARIANNE: I didn't attend Mary Baldwin's School for
Young –

ELINOR: I left when we had no more money!! (*Beat*.) What are
you bringing this up for?

MARIANNE: I just don't think one should be cavalier with
people's lives and feelings, Elinor. That's what I believe.
In fact that is the very basis of all I believe. So when
someone –

ELINOR: Right. (*Laughs. To* EDWARD) Eddie, ask her about
freshman year. A certain Saturday at Lyman House, the
plant house.

EDWARD: I thought I was supposed to stay out –

MARIANNE: We've been through that before, Elinor. I told you
what I remember. I apologized. I was a freshman.

ELINOR: She walks into Lyman –

MARIANNE: Elinor!!

ELINOR: I'm going to tell him! I'm working there on my work
study. I'm watering the plants. And she comes in with
these boys.

MARIANNE: They were from Amherst. Friends, some friends
of someone my father was driving for!! I didn't know any
better. I realized later they were only there to have a good
time with a chauffeur's daughter. They got me drunk –

ELINOR: She comes in drunk, that's right.

MARIANNE: That's rich people for you!!

ELINOR: And for the hell of it, kicks over my water bucket! And then she laughs! All I say is – hey, watch it, and she starts screaming at me like *I'm* some servant!! Don't deny this. You can't deny this happened.

MARIANNE: I was drunk! This was the third week of freshman year!!

ELINOR: So – I'm the rich person. (*Beat.*) Your father didn't think he had to shoot himself in the head because he couldn't pay what he owed to a lot of rich people!! (*Short pause.*) I had nothing in college. (*Beat.*) I had nothing since that happened to Dad. (*Short pause.*) Get off my back. Who's bid is it?

EDWARD: I forget.

ELINOR: I'll deal again.

(*Pause.*)

MARIANNE: *Before* our freshman year . . .

ELINOR: What??

MARIANNE: I received a little note from the dean's office saying that a certain Elinor Blair would be my roommate. Isn't that true?

ELINOR: You never mentioned this –

MARIANNE: When I got to Smith, I find that Miss Blair had asked for another roommate –

ELINOR: A friend of my cousin's. Someone I actually knew –

MARIANNE: Because, as I understand it – and of course no one actually said this – Miss Blair did not want an Italian for a room–

ELINOR: That's not true.

MARIANNE: So who do I get in her place? The only other Italian in the whole freshman class. You think that was a coincidence?

ELINOR: There were other Italians –

MARIANNE: You counted, I'm sure.

ELINOR: That had nothing to do with me. Why would I care if you were –

MARIANNE: I was told it was true!!

ELINOR: Who told you?

50

(*Short pause.*)

MARIANNE: I don't remember any more. Some student.

ELINOR: It wasn't true. (*Short pause.*) And I'm very sorry
you've thought these last six years that it ever could have
been true. (*Beat.*) Why you never mentioned –

MARIANNE: I knew it wasn't true any more.

ELINOR: It never was!
(*Pause.* MARIANNE *nods. A sense of sighing all around.*)

EDWARD: (*Finally*) And –

ELINOR: Eddie, please.

EDWARD: No. And, Elinor did not sleep with this professor of
yours.

MARIANNE: Edward –

EDWARD: She told me when you went in.
(MARIANNE *looks at* ELINOR.)

ELINOR: I didn't . . . We went out that one time. Sat at the bar.
I ended up throwing beer in his face. As I said, he's very
confused.

MARIANNE: Why didn't you just say –

ELINOR: I don't know. I should have, I know. I'm sorry.
(*Short pause.*)

MARIANNE: So am I.
(*Short pause. They smile at each other.*)

EDWARD: Why don't we switch to rummy so Marianne can
play?

ELINOR: (*To* MARIANNE) Do you want to?

MARIANNE: I haven't found anything I want to read.
(*She smiles. Horn off.*)

EDWARD: (*Standing up*) There's Thérèse. (*Looks off.*) It is
her.

ELINOR: Finally. (*Looks at her watch.*) Fifty minutes late.

MARIANNE: (*Half under her breath, to* ELINOR) Rich people.

EDWARD: Do we have everything?

ELINOR: I'm not bringing anything but myself.

MARIANNE: That's what she said. Nothing but ourselves. And
that's what she's going to get.
(*They have gone.*)

1986. The OLDER ELINOR *enters from the lake. She hesitates and then sits down.* OLDER EDWARD *hurries in from the house.*

EDWARD: I thought I saw you out here.

    (*No response.*)

    Did you have a pleasant walk? (*Beat.*) Would you like something to eat? I could bring it out here.

ELINOR: I'm just resting.

EDWARD: I'll see what there is.

    (*He hurries off to the house. After a moment* PETER *hurries out, obviously sent by* EDWARD.)

PETER: It's a beautiful lake, isn't it?

ELINOR: I've been here before.

PETER: Of course you have. You lived –

ELINOR: You wouldn't happen to have an aspirin, would you?

PETER: In the house. (*Beat.*) Do you want me to get it?

ELINOR: I'm thinking that, yes.

PETER: (*Starts to go, stops.*) You will stay here? (*Beat.*) So I can bring you the aspirin?

    (*No response.*)

    (*Goes and stops.*) And a glass of water?

ELINOR: Please. Always a step ahead, aren't you?

    (*He goes off. Short pause.* EDWARD *enters carrying* MARIANNE.)

MARIANNE: (*To* EDWARD) What are you doing taking me back out here for? I want to stay inside.

    (*Pause.* MARIANNE *and* ELINOR *look at each other.*)

    (*Finally*) Feeling better, Elinor?

ELINOR: A little, thank you.

MARIANNE: You look just awful.

    (EDWARD *begins to set her down in a chair.*)

    What are you doing?

EDWARD: My arms are falling asleep.

MARIANNE: No, they're not.

ELINOR: (*Standing up*) Excuse me.

    (*She starts to go.*)

EDWARD: (*To* MARIANNE) If you want to run away.

    (MARIANNE *looks at* ELINOR *who stops.*)

MARIANNE: Set me down. Hurry. Then I'll be the first to sit down.

ELINOR: (*Hurries back and sits.*) I'm sitting down!
(*Pause.*)
EDWARD: (*To* ELINOR) I'll see what there is to eat.
(*He goes.*)
ELINOR: Take your time. I'm quite comfortable. It's rather
like I've been sitting here all morning. (*Beat. To*
MARIANNE) Oh dear, did you come to join me?
(*Pause.* MARIANNE *holds Elinor's book.*)
MARIANNE: (*Finally, to* ELINOR) Fascinating book. Have you
read it? (*Beat.*) I understand it's been shortlisted for this
year's Pulitzer for fiction.
ELINOR: (*Beginning to stand*) I'm sorry, but –
MARIANNE: You're right. This isn't the best time or place to
discuss this. (*Beat.*) Later maybe. And in the main house.
(*Short pause.* ELINOR *decides to sit down again.*)
ELINOR: Marianne –
MARIANNE: That is, if you are feeling better. (*Beat.*) Trust me,
dear, I know what a strain being ill puts on one and I
wouldn't dream of criticizing a friend when she is ill.
(*Beat.*) Who would do such a thing as that?
(*Pause.*)
ELINOR: (*Without looking at* MARIANNE) Marianne, I am
deeply sorry you are ill. I would have said that before, but
I simply assumed – (*Beat.*) We've known each other for so
long. But words won't make you –
(*She covers her face in her hands.*)
MARIANNE: You're wasting your time, Elinor. (*Beat.*) That
hasn't worked on me for years. (*Beat.*) I never understood
why people – men especially – could fall for so obvious a –
(*Beat.*) Does Eddie still fall for that, Elinor? There is
nothing wrong with a little manipulation, but hell what
happened to subtlety? I don't know.
ELINOR: (*Looks up, stares at* MARIANNE.) You've gotten so old
and bitter.
MARIANNE: Wise. Wise. (*Beat.*) Perhaps your book is the
perfect expression of its author.
(EDWARD *returns with a drink in his hand, followed by*
PETER *who carries aspirin and water.*)

53

Who was saying just the other day that the only honest
statement expressed in the whole thing was the price?
(*Laughs, turns to* EDWARD.) Do you remember, Eddie?

EDWARD: You were saying it.

MARIANNE: Right.
(*Pause.* ELINOR *turns to* EDWARD *and notices the drink in
his hand.*)

EDWARD: I guess I forgot your food, but I remembered a
drink.
(*He drinks.*)

ELINOR: (*Turns to* MARIANNE) Go ahead and abuse me. I was
well aware that I was setting myself up for abuse by
coming all the way here. (*Beat.*) Peter, is that my aspirin?
(*He gives it to her.*)
Thank you, dear.
(*She takes it, drinks from the glass, sits back, and rubs her
head. Short pause.*)
I have such a headache.

MARIANNE: Maybe it's brain cancer and you caught it from
me.
(*Pause.*)

ELINOR: Eddie, what I don't understand about Marianne's suit
– We are here to talk about the law suit, are we not?
(*Beat.*) That is the only reason I came here.

EDWARD: I'd hoped we'd get around to that, yes, Elinor.

ELINOR: Here's what I don't understand – Peter, maybe you
can help me understand, as you, like Eddie, are an
intelligent man.

MARIANNE: Will you quit flattering them and talk?!
(*Short pause.*)

ELINOR: Marianne has said that what I wrote hurt her. And
that I hurt her on purpose. (*Beat.*) This thinking misses
completely the kind of book this is. This aims to be.
(*Beat.*) And I'm not saying this is a perfect book – which
perfectly satisfies its goals. Far from it, actually. The
reviewer for the *Post Book Review* had a few grumbles
that I, for one, totally agree with. (*Beat.*) We can only try
to do our best. If there is anything in life I have learned –

(*Short pause.*) My book was not meant to be merely – simply – a life story. (*Beat.*) This is the mistake that Marianne makes. My book is a history. And as a history it attempts to present a world, a time of the world, and a place in that world, from a particular perspective. (*Beat.*) In other words I had points to make.

MARIANNE: Axes to grind.

ELINOR: Points I wished to make about our time. And this from a definite point of view. (*Beat.*) I admit I have a point of view. Marianne has a point of view. And they no doubt are different. And so within a discussion of history in which one is attempting to present the case of one particular point of view – examples, specifics, become unavoidable. (*Beat.*) This is what Marianne has misunderstood. In my book I use Marianne only as an example of a larger idea. She is not the idea itself. She is not the reason for the discussion. My intention was not to criticize her. To hurt her. (*Beat.*) In fact, anyone who knows me knows it is totally against my nature to purposely go out of my way to hurt –

MARIANNE: Eddie, I don't know what she's talking about. Here, read from this page, will you?
(*She hands him the book.*)

ELINOR: Wait. If you don't understand, let me try to make my defence a little clearer, as I believe the whole case rests on –

EDWARD: Defence? What are you talking about? We're sitting outside, having a nice relaxed –

PETER: I think what she's telling us, Edward, is that she has a lawyer –

ELINOR: More than one.

PETER: And that legally, according to libel law, Marianne, as a public figure, is going to have to prove intention to harm. Is that correct?

ELINOR: Yes, it is. That has been my advice.

MARIANNE: It won't stand up in court!

ELINOR: Let's go and see!
(*She stands up.*)

55

PETER: Wait a minute, Elinor. The real problem, in my
    opinion, with this defence is whether Marianne is a public
    figure or not. If not then –
ELINOR: Of course she's –
MARIANNE: Who knows me? Nobody knows –
ELINOR: President emeritus of Bryn Mawr –
MARIANNE: If my work as an educator is so important, why
    didn't you put it in the book? There's not one mention –
EDWARD: Peter!!
    (*They quiet down.*)
PETER: Right. Edward's right. Let's leave the law to the
    lawyers. We're here to have a totally open and general
    discussion of the problem. (*Beat. To* EDWARD) Sorry.
EDWARD: You're a real-estate lawyer!
PETER: I was just trying to help. I said I was sorry. (*Short
    pause. To* MARIANNE) What did you want Edward to read?
EDWARD: (*Handing the book back to* MARIANNE) You read it.
    You read what you want to Elinor.
MARIANNE: I thought you were here to support me.
EDWARD: I am supporting you. (*Beat.*) I'm supporting this
    whole thing. Read what you want to Elinor.
MARIANNE: Coward.
EDWARD: I'm supporting you by trying to get you two talking
    to each other. I think that's a lot of support. (*Beat.*)
MARIANNE: (*To* ELINOR) He always was a coward. No spine.
    Was he with you too?
ELINOR: (*To* MARIANNE) It was terrible. I had a friend who
    called him Eddie Jelly.
MARIANNE: That was me.
ELINOR: I finally couldn't take it. I mean, if you put a drink in
    his hand, at least then he can talk a good fight –
MARIANNE: He has a drink in his hand.
ELINOR: I talk about people like him in the book. He's
    symptomatic of a lot of academic liberals I know. He's
    part of a whole chapter of ex-radical men I have known.
MARIANNE: That chapter I liked.
    (*Pause.* EDWARD *smiles.*)
    I'll read a passage then. (*Beat. Reads from the book:*)

'And then there's Marianne Rinaldi, a very old friend. To be sure, Marianne is an intelligent woman and as a young woman one of my circle of leftist friends.' (*Beat.*) 'Today, her roots in radicalism can hardly be discerned; not a declared conservative, rather that breed of anti-communist liberal whose moral contradictions have long since been well established but who has hung on to the accoutrements of a political philosophy fashionable under John F. Kennedy.' (*Beat.*) 'There is the well-appointed upper West Side apartment – rent-controlled of course – subscriptions to one or two of the more intellectual theatres – such as they are – the house in the Adirondacks – much less showy than one in Connecticut or on the Shore, but also twice as large – which recalls a more pastoral time when socializing the land was the topic instead of today when it is learning how to water-ski when you are sixty-eight.' (*Beat. To* EDWARD) That refers to you.

EDWARD: I know. I know. I read the book.

MARIANNE: (*Reads:*) 'There are the bookcases filled with the *Times* bestseller lists of the last decade, and the endearing maid, Ethel, who has been like a "sister" to Marianne for years.'
(*Short pause. She closes the book.*)

EDWARD: You'll lose your place.

MARIANNE: I have it marked. (*Beat.*) I come off like a hypocrite. You may not have meant that, Elinor, but I do. Did you mean that? Is that what you think? (*Beat.*) I am not a hypocrite! What about *your* possessions?!!!

ELINOR: I do not hide my property in the book, Marianne. I make everything I have very clear, and even confess that for a few things I harbour very strong feelings. But on the whole I make the point that I have not lived for my possessions, I –

MARIANNE: And I have?

ELINOR: Your type has, yes. (*Beat.*) *I* think. (*Beat.*) Maybe not, actually. But I was using you to define a type.

MARIANNE: You attack a friend, a fifty-year-old friendship, to make a point about a type? That doesn't make sense to me. (*Beat.*) When I read this book it did not make sense to me.

ELINOR: It was an important point to make I thought. (*Short pause.*) Marianne, I criticize myself throughout the book. In fact, one could even read it as an act of self-criticism.

MARIANNE: With the subtitle, 'Elinor Blair, Heroine of Our Time'.

ELINOR: It's 'Elinor Blair, A Woman in Our Times'. (*Beat.*) If I really wanted to hurt you – Did you read the chapter on Vietnam? I talked about a cocktail party? I didn't name names. I chose not to name names, but that was your cocktail party, remember? (*Short pause.*) I was late and I came in saying did you hear about what happened at Kent State. And no one had. And I said – 'They are now murdering our children!' (*Beat.*) We then spent – You then spent the whole evening arguing if 'murder' was the right word; that perhaps all we knew for certain was that a 'killing' had taken place and not a 'murder'. (*Beat.*) I never got such a headache in my life. If I really wanted to attack you –

MARIANNE: Attack for what? (*Beat.*) I remember you sitting there half-crocked, sobbing on somebody's knee. 'My children!' What children? You don't have any children! (*Beat.*) The closest you had was the eighteen-year-old co-ed George was seeing on the sly. (*To* EDWARD) She was one of George's students. I held her hand through the whole thing. George was going to leave her.

ELINOR: I don't want to make this into a personal thing.

MARIANNE: Aren't you a little late?

ELINOR: My point was only that you sat there – debating definitions while the other people were out in the street making something happen. (*Beat.*) If it had been left up to you there would still be a Vietnam.

MARIANNE: And there still is a Vietnam, thanks to us. Who do you think kept Johnson's people from blowing up the whole place?!

ELINOR: And being such pals of Johnson that's why you supported Humphrey. You loved Humphrey.

(*She laughs.*)

MARIANNE: I supported McCarthy and you know it. I
supported Kennedy and then I supported McCarthy.

ELINOR: Not in the election.

MARIANNE: McCarthy wasn't in the election. You wanted
Nixon?

ELINOR: We got Nixon.

MARIANNE: No thanks to me. Maybe to you. But not to me.

ELINOR: I don't want to talk just elections. Elections are
meaningless.

MARIANNE: Now you do sound like a communist.

ELINOR: There are worse things to sound like.

MARIANNE: (*Laughs; to* EDWARD) She never learns! (*Beat.*)
But I want to get back to your book.
(*She opens the book.*)

ELINOR: So I used her name. Big deal.

MARIANNE: Why did you do it?

ELINOR: I thought I needed to be specific. Have examples.

MARIANNE: It's like you were getting even for something.
What were you getting even for?

ELINOR: I was making a point! Don't you understand that? I
had no reason. This was not personal. Everything isn't
personal!!!
(*Suddenly* MARIANNE *sort of flinches in pain.*)
Are you all right?

MARIANNE: I'm fine.
(*Beat.*)

ELINOR: (*To the others*) She's probably faking it.

MARIANNE: That's right, I'm faking it.

ELINOR: Just like that quote unquote heart attack she had in
the mid-fifties. Right after she let that teacher be fired.
(*Beat.*) Right after they forced you to let him go. And you
succumbed. (*Beat.*) I remember that. Do you? We all took
great notice of that. That wasn't a heart attack. I'm not
sure you're even sick now.

EDWARD: Elinor –

MARIANNE: No, Edward. She's right. I am just fine. I have
been faking it. I'm fine! (*Beat.*) Now that you know – I

can stop pretending. (*Beat.*) It also means I don't have to pull my punches with you any more, Elinor. Because I don't need your sympathy. I am not sick. (*Beat.*) Let's talk politics some more. (*Beat. Opening the book*) Before we get back to me, let's talk Stalin, Elinor.

ELINOR: I see we've put to rest the witch-hunted teacher . . .

MARIANNE: Did you know him? (*Beat.*) A very gentle good man. Had I left with him, he'd have had nothing. By staying I got him a year's severance.

ELINOR: So you fired him for his own good. Oh, Marianne –

MARIANNE: At the time it was the best option I had. The most sensitive and sensible option!

ELINOR: Sensitive to whom and what?!

MARIANNE: (*Reading:*) '. . . equating Marxism with Stalinism, a ploy used by even those one-time friends of socialism, to taint one and all with the sins of Stalin.' (*She looks up.*) 'The sins of Stalin.' You don't want to go any further than just 'sins'? (*Quickly turns to another marked page.*) (*Reads:*) '. . . Stalinism was as much a cultural movement in the course of Russian history, as it was the result of one man's quest for authoritarian control . . .' (*She starts to turn to another marked page.*)

ELINOR: Read the rest.

(MARIANNE *turns back.*)

MARIANNE: (*Reads:*) '. . . authoritarian control. A nation's propensity for self-disfigurement can, I believe, be called "cultural", but should in no way diminish the destruction wrought by Stalinism itself.' (*Beat.*) Not exactly a disclaimer. (*Turns to another page. Reads:*) 'Nixon, like Joseph Stalin, looked for bodies to throw into the path of –'

ELINOR: (*To* EDWARD) Listen to her, now she's defending Nixon! I knew this would happen.

MARIANNE: (*Throws the book on the table*) Excuses! Smoke-screens! Clouded comparisons! Do you never learn?!

ELINOR: I am not a communist, Marianne. You know that. I never have been. All of a sudden, anyone to your left, you call a –

60

MARIANNE: I call stupid. (*Beat.*) Have some sense, woman. Grow up. The world's not like you thought.

ELINOR: So it's like what? (*Pause.*) Stalin I have never defended.

MARIANNE: You've defended his defenders.

ELINOR: Good writers, teachers. Not because they were anyone's defenders. Friends. (*Beat.*) I couldn't just cut off people. That's not how I am. When someone's a friend – (*Pause.*) That is not how I see the world. I went to Russia.

MARIANNE: Right. (*Laughs. To* EDWARD) On a USIA trip. As a last-minute substitute. And you went because George had two weeks of lectures in Chicago, and you didn't want to stay home alone!

ELINOR: That was not the reason.

MARIANNE: That's what she told me!
(*She laughs.*)

ELINOR: I had many reasons for going.

MARIANNE: So pure. So committed. So ridiculous.

ELINOR: Are you going to throw everything I've ever said back in my face, as if it were the God's honest truth and the real motivation for anything I've done!!?

MARIANNE: What are friends for? (*Beat.*) You've taught me that. Here. (*Picks up the book and taps it, and then opens it. Reads:*) 'Chapter Twenty One: Living with Dying.'

ELINOR: I don't even mention you in that –

MARIANNE: (*To* EDWARD) I read this first in the *Times* magazine. Laughed myself silly. (*Beat.*) She spends a couple of months holding George's hand – how many nurses did he have to actually take care of him? Three, wasn't it? She holds his hand and suddenly she's an expert on the dying.

ELINOR: Obviously not such an expert as you yourself are now.
(*Pause.*)

PETER: (*To* EDWARD, *is if saying this should now be stopped*) Edward –
(EDWARD *saying nothing, and watches.*)

MARIANNE: You have to turn everything into a statement. A commitment, Elinor. (*Beat.*) Everything needs to be

61

something big. George dies. That has to signify
something. (*Beat*.) Can't it just count for what it was?
ELINOR: And what was that?

(*Short pause*.)

MARIANNE: Your husband died. You are old. (*Beat*.) I may go
first. But you'll have to follow.
ELINOR: I see. And that comforts you, does it?
MARIANNE: It doesn't keep me up at night.
ELINOR: Perhaps after you're gone, Eddie and I will get back
together. Two lonely single people. (*Beat*.) Who've
known each other – (*Beat*.) Does that comfort you?
MARIANNE: We've shared men all our life. There was George.
ELINOR: That I do not believe.

(*Short pause*. MARIANNE *smiles*. ELINOR *turns to* EDWARD
who shrugs.)

He would not have done that.

(MARIANNE *snickers and begins looking through the book*.)
This bitterness fascinates me. Perhaps I'll write about it
once you're dead. (*Beat*.) Add a chapter. For the
paperback edition. (*Beat*.) You hadn't thought of that:
who's going to have the last say.

MARIANNE: (*Without looking up*) Marry her, Edward. Marry
and then poison her. Call it a mercy killing, our friends
will know whose mercy you mean. (*She has found the page
in the book. Reads:*) 'What happened to radicalism? If you
were to ask a Marianne Rinaldi today, would she simply
respond with a listing of her recent contributions to
Amnesty International, The Sierra Club, and the ACLU?
In a recent conversation, she talked proudly to me about
having positively refused to use Saran Wrap, the plastic
kitchen wrap, a product of Dow Chemical, the maker of
napalm, since 1967, and about her stand against Barclays
Bank and its association with South African business.
Though she did not say that the closest branch of Barclays
New York was eighty-two blocks from her apartment,
thus there was little fear of this stand causing much
inconvenience . . .' (*Pause. She closes the book*.) Saran
Wrap. Something I mentioned in passing. We were

making coffee in the kitchen together. You complained
about the plastic wrap I had. You said I was cheap. I was
not making a political point to you.

ELINOR: Then who were you making it to?

(*Short pause.*)

MARIANNE: As for Barclays. We were going to Britain for that
summer. You could get their traveller's cheques
anywhere. I was making a point of not buying *them*.
(*Beat.*) You make me sound – Those were not important
things.

(*Short pause.*)

ELINOR: Where did I lie? (*Beat.*) Why have you sued me?
(*Pause.*) I'm not saying I'm any better, Marianne.

MARIANNE: (*Smiles*) Next time you write a book write that in.
'I'm not saying I'm any better, Marianne.'

ELINOR: I thought I did.

(MARIANNE *flinches in pain.*)

Marianne??

(MARIANNE *holds up her hand, to say she is all right.*)

MARIANNE: Where were we?

ELINOR: After the war you thought Eisenhower would make a
great Democrat.

MARIANNE: Let's talk about Hungary. And Poland. And
Czechoslovakia!!! Let's talk Afghanistan!!!!

SCENE 11

Projection: 7.40 p.m.

*The lawn. 1986. A few kerosene lamps are on though the sun is still
up.* PETER *is alone; he leans against the back of a chair, looking
out over the lake. In the distance a loon calls.* EDWARD *comes on
from the direction of the house. Pause.*

EDWARD: Hear the loons?

(PETER *turns to him.*)

They're a regular feature of this place. Always have been.
(*He goes and sits down.*)

PETER: I'm sorry, Edward.

63

(EDWARD *shrugs*.)

EDWARD: Have you eaten anything?

PETER: I don't think I could. (*Beat*.) Not after that boat ride.

EDWARD: It was the boat ride that upset your stomach? (*Beat*.)
You have a strong stomach.

(*Awkward pause*.)

(*Distracted*) Did I thank you for getting the doctor? I
could not have done that any more.

(*Short pause*. PETER *nods his 'you're welcome'*.)

PETER: I've been calling around for a hospital bed. I've got a lead
on two. The doctor thought – We've assumed you don't want
to take her to a hospital. What would be the point?

EDWARD: I hope you called Barbara and – What's my godson's
name again?

PETER: Sean. (*Beat*.) They send their sympathies. I will stay
as long as you need me.

EDWARD: What a terrific life you must lead. Real-estate
lawyer. Wife. Handsome, what? He must be ten years old
by now.

PETER: Fifteen.

EDWARD: Time flies. (*Beat*.) You think I should have stopped
all that.

PETER: A disagreement wasn't the cause. The stroke could
have happened at any time. I asked the doctor.

EDWARD: You asked the doctor? You were afraid we'd killed
her? (*Beat. Looks up at* PETER.) But it wasn't an easy thing
to watch.

PETER: No. (*Beat*.) And half the time I didn't even know what
they were fighting about. Seemed like they were splitting
hairs. Both seem to have beliefs that are so much further
to the left than the vast majority in this –

EDWARD: Peter.

(*Short pause*.)

PETER: That's just an impression, for whatever it's worth.

EDWARD: It's not worth anything.

(PETER *looks away*.)

Sorry. It's just that you can't understand and I have no
patience for listening to ignorant opinions right now. (*Gets

out of the chair.) I should go see how Elinor's holding up. They are best friends.

(*He walks off towards the cabins. After a beat,* PETER *goes off towards the house.*)

1937. The YOUNGER EDWARD *and* ELINOR *enter holding up* YOUNGER MARIANNE, *who is pale and trying not to vomit.*

ELINOR: We're almost there.

MARIANNE: I feel . . .

ELINOR: We know how you feel.

EDWARD: It was a rough boat ride.

ELINOR: Eddie, she drank too much. I told her she was drinking too much. I'm surprised her stomach's made it this far.

(MARIANNE *grabs her stomach.*)

I have you. (*To* EDWARD) I'll take her, Eddie.

(*She takes her towards the cabins.*)

We'll get something cold on your face. Hold on to me, I've got you.

(*They go. Pause.* EDWARD *suddenly notices the kerosene lamps on and smiles. He looks towards the house.*)

EDWARD: (*Calls:*) Gene! Gene! (*As he runs off*) You're back!!!

SCENE 12

Projection: Night.
The lawn.
1986. EDWARD *sits to one side, finishing a drink. More lanterns have been lit.*
1937. EDWARD *and* ELINOR *sit.* EDWARD *is laughing.* ELINOR *looks at him. After a moment,* MARIANNE *enters from the direction of the cabins.*

MARIANNE: What?

ELINOR: How do you feel? He's not laughing at you.

MARIANNE: I'm OK. (*Beat.*) I thought I was counting my drinks. (*Beat.*) I guess I was nervous. I'm sorry if I embarrassed –

ELINOR: Nervous about what?

MARIANNE: I don't know. (*Beat.*) I guess rich people make me both angry and nervous.

EDWARD: Rich people can go to hell for all I care.

(MARIANNE *looks to* ELINOR, *realizing something has happened*.)

ELINOR: He talked to Gene.

MARIANNE: He's back? Where's he been?

(EDWARD *just laughs and rubs his eyes*.)

ELINOR: (*After first looking to* EDWARD) Gene was in the city. He'd remembered some business. (*Beat.*) He said he – Well, Eddie has the feeling that he just sort of forgot about us. Actually, when Eddie called to him on the porch, when we just got back – there was a moment when –

EDWARD: (*Still rubbing his eyes; without looking at anyone*) It seemed like he didn't even recognize me. I think for a second he thought I was a neighbour.

MARIANNE: I don't believe this. I thought he was your good –

EDWARD: So did I.

(*Pause.*)

ELINOR: We're leaving tomorrow morning.

MARIANNE: You won't get an argument out of me.

ELINOR: We have to leave. (*Beat.*) It seems Gene had invited some other friends to come tomorrow.

MARIANNE: You're joking?

(EDWARD *laughs*.)

EDWARD: (*Laughing*) He'd forgotten that he'd invited them.

ELINOR: After he saw Edward he said he'd forgotten he'd invited them.

MARIANNE: So he's kicking us out.

EDWARD: (*Laughing*) He said he could get us reservations at an inn in the town. He didn't offer to pay.

MARIANNE: He's –

ELINOR: We're not done. His friends whom he'd forgotten he'd invited at the same time he had invited us – whom we know he also forgot about – they are sort of a leftist theatre group. A readers' theatre group. (*Beat.*) They're talking to Gene about him helping them out.

(*Beat.*)

EDWARD: (*Smiling*) But he said not to worry, he wasn't planning
on giving them a dime. So I shouldn't feel like I was in some
sort of competition – He said that when people approach
him for money he finds it very hard to say no. (*Beat.*) He's
learned not to say yes. He just can't say no.

ELINOR: Edward tried to give him a copy of the editorial
statement.

MARIANNE: He didn't even –

ELINOR: No. He didn't. When you tried what?

(EDWARD *does not respond.*)

Gene said he was tired. He was going to bed. He doesn't
read in bed. (*Beat.*) Eddie still has the copy, don't you,
Eddie? He wouldn't even touch it. What did he say? He
said – well, if we wanted our best chance, then, we should
be patient and wait. (*Beat.*) He suggests we take our lead
from him. He'd let us know. (*Beat.*) Don't call us, we'll
call –

EDWARD: (*Suddenly stands and screams towards the house:*) You
son of a bitch!!!!!

(*Pause.* EDWARD *sits back down.*)

MARIANNE: Eddie?

(*He turns to her.*)

I told you so.

(*He flinches.*)

ELINOR: She did, Eddie. We both did, but you wouldn't listen.
You knew better.

MARIANNE: You wouldn't listen to anyone –

EDWARD: Look, I feel stupid enough already! Please.

(*Pause.*)

ELINOR: (*Getting up*) I'm going to take a walk. See how the lake
looks. Maybe go swimming. (*To* MARIANNE) You want to
come?

MARIANNE: It's dark.

ELINOR: Take a lantern.

MARIANNE: (*Getting up*) Why not? Might help me feel better.

EDWARD: (*Turns on her*) Don't blame me for *that*! I didn't make
you drink too much!

(*Beat.*)

MARIANNE: No. No, you didn't. (*Beat.*) Thank you for reminding me of that.

EDWARD: What are friends for?

(*Short pause. He gets up and starts toward the house;* ELINOR *and* MARIANNE *are taking down a lantern.*)

(*Stops, turns back.*) Elinor?

(*She turns.*)

May I join you two? (*Beat.*) Gene's at the window. I guess he heard me. I better not go in there right now.

(*Short pause.*)

ELINOR: Marianne?

MARIANNE: Sure. What are friends for?

(*They take the lantern and go off towards the lake. The* OLDER EDWARD *laughs to himself and mumbles 'What are friends for?' The* OLDER ELINOR *enters from the house.*)

ELINOR: What? Who are you talking to?

EDWARD: I was daydreaming.

ELINOR: (*Noticing his empty drink*) You want another drink? I'll go back in –

EDWARD: Peter can do that.

(*She sits.*)

He was going to talk to her brother. I thought he should hear. (*Beat.*) I suppose we should call Bryn Mawr. They would want to know. She was such a force there.

(*Pause.*)

ELINOR: (*Sighs*) You can't sit in there forever.

EDWARD: No.

ELINOR: Why can't the dead just die?

(EDWARD *turns to her.*)

She seems comfortable.

(*From the distance the sound of people swimming and talking, even laughing.*)

What's that?

EDWARD: Kids down the lake. There's a new cabin down there. They have kids. They must be out swimming.

ELINOR: You never used to hear anything.

(PETER *enters with a couple of drinks.* EDWARD *is startled.*)

EDWARD: What?!

PETER: Her brother's flying into Albany.

EDWARD: Oh. (*Beat. To* ELINOR) I thought – (*To* PETER) Don't scare me. Don't hurry around like that.

PETER: I thought you'd both like a drink.

(*They take their drinks.*)

I thought I'd call Bryn Mawr. Leave a message at the switchboard at least. Someone there should be told.

EDWARD: Good idea, Peter. You're a smart fellow. We would never have thought of that ourselves.

(ELINOR *smiles.* PETER *goes back inside. Long pause.*)

I've been thinking about your book, Elinor.

ELINOR: I –

EDWARD: I'm talking. Let me finish. (*Short pause.*) I think she would have died five, six months ago if you hadn't written about her like you did. You got her so angry – (ELINOR *smiles.*) That book kept her alive. (*He smiles. Short pause.*) I've wondered if maybe that's why you wrote about her like that. To get her angry. You know her better than anyone else, Elinor, and I'll bet you thought – if I could only get her fighting – (*Beat.*) That could keep her living. (*Beat.*) So you –

ELINOR: No, Eddie.

EDWARD: Even if it were unconscious on your part, still –

ELINOR: No.

(*Pause. She reaches for his hand.*)

Yes. That's why.

(*He nods, takes a sip of his drink; she tries to fight back tears.*)

EDWARD: The funeral will be at Riverside.

(ELINOR *nods; she does not look at him.*)

She always said she didn't want a memorial service.

(*Short pause.*)

ELINOR: (*Takes a sip*) When I get back to the city, I'll begin to arrange for one.

EDWARD: Good.

(*Pause.*)

ELINOR: I look forward to that. It'll be interesting to see who's left.

(*Pause.*)